Identifying and Managing Acquisition and Sustainment Supply Chain Risks

Nancy Y. Moore, Elvira N. Loredo, Amy G. Cox, Clifford A. Grammich

RAND Project AIR FORCE

Prepared for the United States Air Force
Approved for public release; distribution unlimited

For more information on this publication, visit www.rand.org/t/RR549

Library of Congress Cataloging Number: 2014958838
ISBN: 978-0-8330-8609-9

Published by the RAND Corporation, Santa Monica, Calif.

© Copyright 2015 RAND Corporation

RAND® is a registered trademark.

Limited Print and Electronic Distribution Rights

This document and trademark(s) contained herein are protected by law. This representation of RAND intellectual property is provided for noncommercial use only. Unauthorized posting of this publication online is prohibited. Permission is given to duplicate this document for personal use only, as long as it is unaltered and complete. Permission is required from RAND to reproduce, or reuse in another form, any of its research documents for commercial use. For information on reprint and linking permissions, please visit www.rand.org/pubs/permissions.html.

The RAND Corporation is a research organization that develops solutions to public policy challenges to help make communities throughout the world safer and more secure, healthier and more prosperous. RAND is nonprofit, nonpartisan, and committed to the public interest.

RAND's publications do not necessarily reflect the opinions of its research clients and sponsors.

Support RAND
Make a tax-deductible charitable contribution at
www.rand.org/giving/contribute

www.rand.org

Preface

In recent years, the Air Force and, particularly, its suppliers have pursued various ways to improve performance, reduce costs, and otherwise adopt best industry practices. These include outsourcing, global sourcing, supply base rationalization, single sourcing, just-in-time deliveries, and lean inventories. Although these practices offer many benefits in efficiency and effectiveness, they can also make supply chains more brittle and increase the risks of supply disruptions.

This report examines supply chain risk management, including evolving commercial and Air Force practices, and makes recommendations for modifying Air Force practices. The research was performed as part of a project titled "Identifying and Managing Risks Associated with Agile Supply Chains," conducted in RAND Project AIR FORCE's Resource Management Program and commissioned by the Director of Transformation, Deputy Chief of Staff for Logistics, Installations, and Mission Support; Deputy Assistant Secretary for Acquisition Integration, Office of the Assistant Secretary of the Air Force for Acquisition; and Deputy Assistant Secretary of the Air Force for Logistics, Office of the Assistant Secretary of the Air Force for Installations, Environment, and Logistics. After this research was completed, the Air Force reorganized the Air Force Materiel Command. The new structure established an Air Force Life Cycle Management Center (AFLCMC) and an Air Force Sustainment Center (AFSC). The AFLCMC consolidates product development and support system design. The AFSC integrates depot maintenance and Air Force supply chain activities. The findings and recommendations presented in this report are relevant to how the Air Force will identify and manage supply chain risk under the new organizational structure.

Work on this project occurred in two phases. The first phase reviewed sustainment supply chain risks and was documented in Nancy Y. Moore and Elvira N. Loredo, *Identifying and Managing Air Force Sustainment Supply Chain Risks*, Santa Monica, Calif.: RAND Corporation DB-649-AF, 2013. This work summarizes research on both sustainment supply chain risks and supply chain risks that can be addressed during acquisition processes. Work presented here on sustainment supply chain risks heavily leverages our earlier publication.

This research should be of interest to those purchasing and providing goods and services to the Air Force.

RAND Project Air Force

RAND Project AIR FORCE (PAF), a division of the RAND Corporation, is the U.S. Air Force's federally funded research and development center for studies and analyses. PAF provides the Air Force with independent analyses of policy alternatives affecting the development, employment, combat readiness, and support of current and future air, space, and cyber forces. Research is conducted in four programs: Force Modernization and Employment; Manpower, Personnel, and Training; Resource Management; and Strategy and Doctrine. The research reported here was prepared under contract FA7014-06-C-0001.

Additional information about PAF is available on our website:
http://www.rand.org/paf/

Contents

Figures

Tables

Summary

In recent years, the Air Force and, particularly, its suppliers have pursued various ways to improve performance, reduce costs, and otherwise adopt best industry practices. Several of these may introduce new sources of risk to the supply chain, or at least risks that the Air Force is not accustomed to addressing. In this report, we discuss how the Air Force might address these risks. We review the origins of these risks, discuss ways that private industry and the Air Force have addressed risks, devise a composite process for managing risks, and note prototype maps that Air Force personnel may wish to develop to better manage risks. We find that Air Force supply chain risk management lags that of industry, but we offer suggestions that can remedy this.

Our work has several components. We reviewed the emerging literature on supply chain risk management. We conducted a series of interviews with acquisition and sustainment personnel, representatives of Air Force commodity councils, Defense Logistics Agency personnel, and representatives of a Contractor Logistics Support contract and high-technology companies on their approaches to managing supply chain risks. Finally, we developed prototype examples of maps that the Air Force may wish to use in identifying and managing supply chain risks.

Risk Trends

The Air Force has faced three trends that, unaddressed, could ultimately increase its supply chain risks.

First, the Air Force and, particularly, its suppliers have pursued various means to improve performance, reduce costs, and otherwise adopt best industry practices. These include outsourcing, global sourcing, supply base rationalization, single sourcing, just-in-time deliveries, and lean inventories. Although these offer many benefits in efficiency and effectiveness, they can also make supply chains more brittle and, consequently, increase an enterprise's exposure to supply disruptions, particularly those in the upstream supply chain.

Second, within the Air Force, the increasingly sophisticated technology and integration of Air Force weapon systems, coupled with outsourcing by original equipment manufacturers, further underscores the importance of the supply chain and minimizing risks to it.

Third, budget constraints and the increasing costs of new weapons are increasing pressure to reduce force sizes and their support infrastructure. Such reductions are likely to lead to further supplier and organic facility consolidations and possibly more outsourcing. Such consolidation can reduce redundancies but could also increase the likelihood and consequences of supply chain disruptions.

To be sure, these benefits of increased efficiency and effectiveness can outweigh the risks that they introduce to the supply chain—if the risks are addressed. Given the importance to the Air Force and the increasing complexity of external supply chains, the Air Force asked RAND Project AIR FORCE to help it develop an enterprise-wide strategy for proactively managing supply chain risks. We consider not only sustainment processes, in which the effects of supply chains might be most visible, but acquisition processes, in which the Air Force has the greatest opportunities to manage the supply chain risks it faces.

Supply Chain Risk Management

We define supply chain risk management as the coordination of activities to direct and control an enterprise's end-to-end supply chain with regard to supply chain risks. Yet defining exactly where the supply chain starts can vary for different producers. For industry products, supply chain management typically starts with design of a new product, when managers have the greatest number of options, and continues through production to aftermarket support, when there are many fewer supply chain risk management options. Although the development of a new weapon system in the Department of Defense (DoD) has somewhat similar life cycle phases to that for development of a new industry product, within DoD, the extensive focus on supply chain management does not typically start until the sustainment phase. DoD leaves management of many supply chain risks in production to its prime contractors. Table S.1 portrays the approximate phases in industry and DoD product development and shows when the focus on managing supply chains begins.

Regardless of when or how supply chain risk is considered, there are three dimensions for measuring its magnitude. These are

- the likelihood or probability of occurrence of an event that could cause adverse effects, i.e., produce harm or loss
- the expected consequence, that is, what would happen to an enterprise should a risk become reality
- the duration, that is, how long the risk event causes loss or harm to an enterprise.

Enterprises can undertake one of a number of traditional buffering strategies to deal with new supply chain risks, but these traditional strategies also have risks. For example,

Table S.1. Key Differences in When Industry and DoD Use the Term "Supply Chain Management"

Industry→Product	DoD→Weapon System
Design—supply chain management typically starts here	Acquisition — Design
Production — Supply chain — Assembly	— Manufacturing Original equipment manufacturer (OEM) and its suppliers
Aftermarket support — Supply chain	Sustainment—supply chain management typically starts here[a] — Supply chain

[a]Except cybersecurity initiatives, for which supply chain management typically starts in design.

using multiple sources of supply can limit price leverage and increase variance in quality and delivery time. Using frequent and extensive competition can limit opportunities for collaboration and continuous improvement. Expediting orders increases their total costs. Increasing order quantities can induce a "bullwhip effect," amplifying demand as orders move up the supply chain. Maintaining inventory safety stocks also increases total costs. Maintaining a well-stocked supply pipeline can both increase total costs and hide supply chain problems.

Overall, the benefits realized from new supply chain management practices increase the importance of new risk management practices, especially practices that shift from risk buffering and reactive management to proactively identifying, understanding, and effectively managing end-to-end supply chain risks and vulnerabilities. Enterprises must identify prospective risks and vulnerabilities to the supply chain, determine their likelihood, and assess their likely consequence.

A Composite Process for Managing Supply Chain Risk

After conducting our interviews and reviewing relevant literature, we identified a composite, multistep, continuous process for supply chain risk management. Figure S.1 outlines this process. We present this process both as a recommendation for the Air Force to consider as well as a standard by which to evaluate current supply chain risk management practices, which we discuss below.

Figure S.1. Supply Chain Risk Management Is a Multistep, Continuous Process

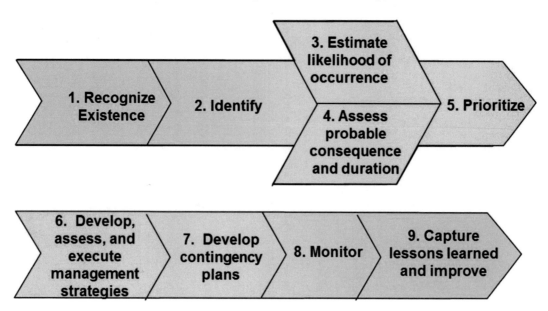

Details for the steps include the following:

1. Recognize the existence of risk. Before an enterprise can address supply risks, it must be aware of its supply vulnerabilities, as well as the possibility that its actions, or inaction, can create supply chain risks.

2. Identify risks. Enterprises must identify the possible risks associated with a supply strategy. Natural disasters, for example, may pose supply chain risks, which enterprises can map. Supplier participation is also necessary to identify as well as mitigate risks.

3. Estimate the likelihood of occurrence. Enterprises may do this by assigning a relative weight to the probability of occurrence or classifying the probability of occurrence into categories such as low, medium, and high.

4. Assess the probable consequences and duration of a risk if one is realized. In this step, concurrent with step 3, enterprises assess the relative total consequence or significance of the prospective loss to calibrate the exposure of the business. The total consequences of a risk are a function of its scale, scope, duration/recovery time, and total cost.

5. Prioritize risks. Few, if any, organizations have the resources to eliminate all risks. Consequently, rather than addressing all vulnerable areas at once, enterprises may focus their supply chain risk management efforts on those events where their efforts are likely to provide the greatest relief. One way the Air Force does this, as Figure S.2 shows, is to plot risks by categories of likelihood and consequence, then to classify these as level A-risk, B-risk, or C-risk.

Figure S.2. A Two-Dimensional Risk Matrix Can Help Prioritize Supply Chain Risk Management Efforts

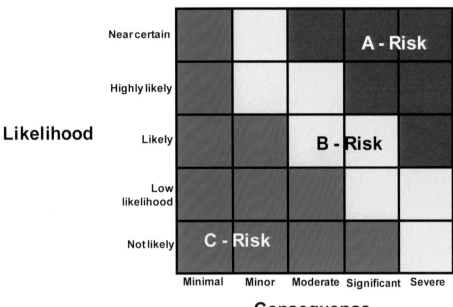

6. Develop, assess, and execute a risk management strategy. The strategies an enterprise develops will depend on the phase of the weapon system's life cycle and the risks it seeks to address. An enterprise may choose to ignore or accept low-priority (C) risks while trying to avoid or reduce the likelihood of a high-priority (A) one.

7. Develop contingency plans. This step focuses on developing contingency plans for disruptions because not all risks can be effectively avoided, adequately mitigated, or even identified. Such plans should focus not on every possible source of disruption but rather on outcomes and how to restore operations in event of a disruption, independent of the source. Contingency plans can help enterprises quickly respond to unforeseen disruptions and thus reduce their total consequences.

8. Monitor continuously. After establishing a supply strategy and risk management plan, organizations should continuously monitor the environment for any change in prospective supply chain risks that warrant modification of the supply strategy or risk management plan.

9. Capture lessons learned and improve. This step focuses on continuous learning and knowledge management. When a supply disruption occurs, an enterprise should conduct postincident audits to determine the cause of the disruption and to document any lessons learned for better managing future events.

DoD and Air Force Guidance for Managing Supply Chain Risk

DoD risk management policies already target many risks identified in the business literature. For example, DoD has policies to manage risks of stock outages, drawdown, or expiration, similar to industry's focus on demand uncertainty or volatility. Like industry, DoD also has policies to manage the risks of supplier financial problems. DoD policies to address risks posed by repair cycle time, order and shipping time, maintenance replacement rate, or resupply from external sources are similar to those in industry to address risks posed by long lead times, logistics delays or failure, and internal risks. Strictly beyond what industry practices, DoD also has policies to address risks posed by underutilization of existing inventory. But it does not have policies for managing a number of supply chain risks such as those posed by environmental risks, natural disasters, pricing, geopolitical events, and other events that are discussed in the business literature.

Many such external supply chain risks that DoD does not consider, and hence only reactively manages, are covered by *force majeure* clauses exempting suppliers from responsibility for disruptions caused by natural disasters, acts of war or terrorism, labor unrest, or "acts of God," among other things. Although such clauses are required in federal contracts by the Federal Acquisition Regulation, their presence in contracts means that DoD and its components, including the Air Force, rather than suppliers, must manage risks posed by such events.

Supply Risks that DoD Personnel Consider

We asked acquisition and sustainment personnel about general and specific risks that they consider in their work, among other topics. Overall, we found that the types of risks that each considers differ substantially.

For example, acquisition personnel are more likely to consider physical and regulatory risks such as material unavailability or regulatory noncompliance, production problems such as lack of capacity or technological inadequacies or failures, financial costs and losses, and management risks such as management quality and upstream supply risks. Acquisition personnel typically considered these risks "always" or "often," whereas sustainment personnel typically considered them "half the time," "rarely," or "never." One reason for this, sustainment personnel told us, is that by the time weapon systems move to sustainment, many parts have only one supplier, and sustainment personnel do not believe that there is much they can do to manage sole- and single-source supplier risks.

Similarly, acquisition personnel "always" or "often" consider buying-enterprise risks such as planning failures and financial uncertainty, whereas sustainment personnel consider these "half the time" or "rarely." Nevertheless, sustainment personnel do consider such buying-enterprise risks as demand volatility, testing unavailability, and market issues about as often as acquisition personnel do.

Acquisition personnel were more likely than sustainment personnel to consider distribution risks, such as cargo damage/theft/tampering and long multiparty supply pipelines. They also reported considering, on average, external risks such as labor unavailability, lawsuits, and technological uncertainty "always or often," whereas sustainment personnel, on average, considered such risks no more than "half the time." Acquisition personnel reported considering external risks such as accidents, natural disasters, and sabotage or terrorism only "half the time," but this was still more often than sustainment personnel considered them. Neither acquisition nor sustainment personnel were likely to consider distribution risks such as infrastructure unavailability, vehicle accidents, or labor unrest or unavailability.

Altogether, we found that supply chain risk management is not consistent across the Air Force and, where it is practiced, it is often not sufficient. Weapon system managers reported a lack of enterprise-wide supply chain risk management procedures and mechanisms. They also differed in the extent to which they considered supply chain risks. Few had mitigation plans for such risks. One reason cited for the lack of a proactive approach to supply chain risk management is the lack of tools for identifying such risks.

Regardless of the differences in how acquisition and sustainment personnel consider supply chain risks, the Air Force needs to consider supply chain risks completely throughout the life of a weapon system. Acquisition personnel consider many risks that they believe they can manage, as do sustainment personnel. This focus on risks that they believe they can manage means that risks neither can manage alone may not always be addressed.

Developing Prototype Supply Chain Risk Management Maps

One way the Air Force can increase its supply chain risk management efforts is to use existing data to map supply chain risks. Google Maps, for example, offers a no-cost way to map locations of interest, and the Federal Procurement Data System offers a way to identify suppliers and associate them with particular locations. Adding data such as hurricane, tornado, or earthquake occurrences and overlaying this information with existing data can help the Air Force identify suppliers, particularly of critical parts, which may be at risk from a natural disaster.

Leading commercial enterprises, for example, map their production and distribution locations, including the products supported by these locations, and link this information to other data. Then, in response to nearly any event around the world, they are able to identify the suppliers and products affected, whether the suppliers will be able to fulfill time-to-recovery commitments, and put contingency plans into place, if necessary, to reduce the duration and consequence of the disruption.

Conclusions and Recommendations

Our findings point to two key recommendations with a number of actionable steps.

First, we recommend that the Air Force develop policies and processes to identify, measure, and assess supply chain risks across weapon systems and over their life cycles. Current policies and processes related to supply chain risk management during acquisition and sustainment are inadequate. Supply chain risk management policy and training ought to be expanded to provide personnel with the direction and capabilities to better manage supply chain risks. Supply chain risk management should be elevated within the acquisition process so that it is not overshadowed by cost, schedule, and technology issues. It needs to be endemic in technology development and identification of manufacturing risks, which do get attention. Consideration of supply chain risk management should be a weapon system program manager's responsibility throughout acquisition and sustainment processes (i.e., through the weapon system life cycle) in addition to costs, schedule, and performance. Last, it should flow up the supply chain from prime contractors to their suppliers and their suppliers' suppliers.

Second, we recommend that the Air Force develop supply chain risk maps to help identify, assess, and manage supply chain risks based on leading industry practices. Air Force personnel do not currently have the visibility and assessment tools they need to adequately identify, assess, and manage supply chain risks. By collaborating with and leveraging companies with more mature supply chain risk management programs, the Air Force can quickly adapt best practices in this area to its own environment.

Acknowledgments

This report would not have been possible without the contributions of many individuals. First, we wish to thank Grover Dunn, then–Director of Transformation, Deputy Chief of Staff for Logistics, Installations and Mission Support (AF/A4I), for supporting this project. We also wish to thank F-16 supply chain management personnel, Boeing personnel, Defense Logistics Agency personnel, a number of different weapon system program management personnel, and personnel at several leading companies for taking time from their busy schedules to answer our interview questions. We also thank the reviewers of the sustainment version of this document, Ellen Pint and Sarah Nowak of RAND, and Stanley Griffis of Michigan State University. Portions of this document draw heavily on that earlier version. In addition, we thank reviewers of this version of the document, including James B. Rice Jr., William Shelton, and Sean Bednarz. Finally, we thank Donna Mead, Megan McKeever, and Jane Siegel for formatting different versions of this draft.

Abbreviations

AAC	Air Armament Center
AAIP	Aircraft Availability and Improvement Program
ADM	acquisition decision memorandum
AFCD	Air Force Capabilities Document
AFI	Air Force Instruction
AFLCMC	Air Force Life Cycle Management Center
AFMC	Air Force Materiel Command
AFROCC	Air Force Requirements for Operational Capabilities Council
AFSC	Air Force Sustainment Center
ALC	Air Logistics Center
AoA	analysis of alternatives
ASC	Aeronautical Systems Center
CAMP	Commodity Acquisition Management Plan
CDR	critical design review
CLS	contractor logistics support
CM	contract manufacturer
CMP	Commodity Management Plan
CNCI	Comprehensive National Cybersecurity Initiative
CoA	course of action
CPD	capability production document
CVCM	Customer Value Chain Management
DAB	Defense Acquisition Board
DCMA	Defense Contract Management Agency
DDR	detail design review
DLA	Defense Logistics Agency
DoD	Department of Defense
DoDD	Department of Defense Directive
DSOR	depot source of repair
DTM	Directive Type Memo
EOA	early operational assessment
ESC	Electronic System Center
FAA	Federal Aviation Administration
FAR	Federal Acquisition Regulation
FDE	full deployment evaluation

FFATA	Federal Funding Accountability and Transparency Act
FOC	full operational capability
FOT&E	follow-on test and evaluation
FPDS	Federal Procurement Data System
FRPDR	full rate production decision review
FSA	functional solutions analysis
FY	fiscal year
GIG	global information grid
GTE	gas-turbine engine
HP	Hewlett-Packard
HSI	human systems integration
ICD	Initial Capabilities Document
ICT	information-communication technology
ILS	Integrated Logistics Support
IOC	initial operational capability
IPT	integrated process team
ISO	International Organization for Standardization
ISP	information support plan
IT	information technology
ITAB	Information Technology Acquisition Board
ITAR	International Traffic in Arms Regulations
JROC	Joint Requirements Oversight Council
LCL	life-cycle logistics
LCMP	life cycle management plan
LFT&E	live fire test and evaluation
LGCC	Landing Gear Commodity Council
LSI	lead system integrator
MDA	Milestone Decision Authority
MGB	Material Governance Board
MS	milestone
OA	operational assessment
OEM	Original equipment manufacturer
OMB	Office of Management and Budget
OSS&E	operational safety, suitability, and effectiveness
OT&E	operational test and evaluation
PBL	performance-based logistics
PDR	preliminary design review
PIR	post implementation review

PMD	program management directive
RSR	requirements strategy review
SAE	Senior Acquisition Executive
SCMW	Supply Chain Management Wing
SCRLC	Supply Chain Risk Leadership Council
SCRM	supply chain risk management
SEP	systems engineering plan
SSOR	strategic source of repair
T&E	test and evaluation
TDS	technology development strategy
TEMP	Test and Evaluation Master Plan
TSP	team software process
TSPSP	Total System Product Support Package

1. Introduction

In recent years, the Air Force and, particularly, its suppliers have pursued various ways to improve performance, reduce costs, and otherwise adopt best industry practices. Several of these may introduce new sources of risk to the supply chain, or at least risks that the Air Force is not accustomed to addressing. In this report, we identify these risks and discuss how the Air Force might address them.

In this chapter, we discuss the various sources of supply chain risks in general and specifically for the Air Force. In Chapter 2, we review definitions of supply chain risk management, we then discuss where supply risks are typically managed in the private sector and the Department of Defense (DoD), trends affecting supply chain risks, more traditional approaches to managing supply chain risks, and perceptions of what constitutes a risk. In Chapter 3, we provide a primer on evolving supply chain risk management practices. Those familiar with supply chain risk management may want to skim these first three chapters before reading our subsequent chapters, which are more specific to DoD.

We begin by reviewing emerging sources of supply chain risks, including how these shift as Air Force weapon system maintenance support shifts from organic (or internal) to contractor-provided (or external) sources. We also review the methods we use to assess current supply chain risk management practices and ways the Air Force can improve them.

Sources of Supply Chain Risks

Among emerging industry practices the Air Force and its suppliers has been adopting are outsourcing, global sourcing, supply base rationalization, single sourcing, just-in-time deliveries, and lean inventories. Many new practices to improve the efficiency and effectiveness of supply chains are increasing their "brittleness" and, consequently, an enterprise's exposure to supply disruptions (Griffin, 2008).

Such challenges increase the importance of securing supply; indeed, in the view of some analysts (e.g., Steele and Court, 1996), securing supply regardless of broader forces in the purchasing environment is the prime task for an effective purchasing organization. Risk management for such organizations consists of examining the entire supply chain for a good or service. This should include both upstream to identify potential future supply problems and downstream to identify potential future distribution and customer problems.

Developing additional sources of supply can help reduce risks, but having them does not necessarily reduce supply chain vulnerabilities. Better options to reduce vulnerabilities may be available by working with existing suppliers, e.g., using dual sites to assure supply at one site should a disaster strike the other, or making sure that suppliers have plans to address a wide variety of contingencies.[1]

The supply chain challenges the Air Force faces are complicated by its changing missions, operations, and requirements for support. With the rise of smaller, regional conflicts and antiterrorist operations has come much more uncertainty regarding Air Force deployments, including their timing, location, and intensity. In response, the Air Force has developed plans and policies that require a very responsive, flexible, and resilient sustainment supply chain for its forces. Furthermore, the rising costs of sophisticated new technologies to counter new threats have driven up the real costs of weapons over time, reducing the numbers that the Air Force can acquire and increasing the consequences of supply chain disruptions (see, for example, Arena et al., 2008).

Fewer weapons and more deployments often lead to much lower densities of weapons at home stations and deployed. These lower densities, in turn, make cannibalization for parts more costly, in terms of both aircraft availability and maintenance hours, and supply chains for weapon parts more important.

The increasingly sophisticated technology and integration of Air Force weapon systems, coupled with outsourcing by original equipment manufacturers (OEMs), further underscores the importance of the supply chain and managing risks to it.[2] Integrated weapon systems can complicate support because they require more sophisticated testing to ensure that all systems interfaces are properly functioning. The F-22, for example, has proven very complex and expensive for the Air Force to operate, with mission-capable rates of about 62 percent, which is below what was expected (Thompson, 2009).

Budget constraints coupled with the increasing costs of new weapons and personnel are increasing pressure to reduce the physical size of and budgets for support infrastructure. This has included Office of Secretary of Defense policies for outsourcing the support of some legacy and many new weapons in so-called performance based logistics (PBL) contracts that optimize system availability and minimize cost and logistics footprint (Department of Defense, undated). Reducing the budget for support infrastructure is likely to lead to consolidation of suppliers and organic facilities and

---

[1] For specific examples of steps to reduce single-source risk, see Nelson, Mayo, and Moody (1998); Chozick (2007); and Kim (2012). For more on supply vulnerability and competitive advantage, see Sheffi (2005); and Sheffi and Rice (2005).

[2] For discussions of similar issues regarding a civilian aircraft, specifically the Boeing 787 "Dreamliner," see Holmes (2007); and "Boeing Acquires Stake in Plant" (2009).

possibly more outsourcing.[3] Consolidation reduces redundancies but could also multiply the effects of a disruption within the supply chain.

Methods of This Study

Given the importance and increasing complexity of external supply chains to the Air Force, the Air Force asked RAND to help it develop an enterprise-wide strategy for proactively managing supply chain risks. In this report, we seek to help the Air Force improve the effectiveness of its "upstream" supply chain risk management (SCRM). We consider not only sustainment processes, in which the effects of supply chains might be most visible, but acquisition processes, in which the Air Force might have the greatest leverage in supply chain arrangements and be best able to mitigate the risks it faces in sustainment supply chains.[4]

We began by reviewing the academic and business literature on supply chain risk management. Because this is an emerging field, the literature is fairly recent and much less developed than literature on other risks or supply chain management generally. We also reviewed Air Force and DoD guidance regarding sustainment supply chain risk identification and management.

To deepen our understanding of supply chain risks for the Air Force and in industries of concern to it, we conducted a series of interviews, using questions based on our reviews of the literature and policy guidance, with personnel involved in supply chain risk management, contracting, and commodity-management issues.

First, we interviewed sustainment personnel involved with two weapon systems: the F-16 and the C-17 aircraft. We chose these two because the F-16 is a legacy weapon system, which primarily has organic support and is now in sustainment rather than acquisition phase, whereas the C-17 is a newer contractor-supported system transitioning from acquisition to sustainment. Appendix A includes the core protocol for these interviews.

These interviews asked respondents to assess the frequency of a variety of risks, as shown in Appendix B. Because commodity councils are responsible for developing

---

[3] The Air Force has retreated somewhat from outsourcing because of higher-than-expected costs and breaching of the "50/50 rule" requiring that at least half of maintenance be performed at a public depot. Congress has also put a moratorium on Office of Management and Budget (OMB) Circular A-76 studies, which are required to outsource civilian jobs (Rooney, 2012). Nevertheless, to the extent that the Air Force continues to outsource support, we can expect its supply chain risks to evolve.

[4] Much of the work on the first phase of our research, regarding sustainment supply chain risks, is documented in Moore and Loredo (2013). This document summarizes research on both sustainment supply chain risks and supply chain risks that can be addressed during acquisition processes. Work presented here on sustainment supply chain risks heavily leverages our earlier publication.

enterprise-wide sustainment supply strategies for most sustainment contracts, we asked three representatives of commodity councils to complete the risk assessment shown in Appendix B as well.[5]

During our interviews, we learned of the importance of the Defense Logistics Agency (DLA) in managing Air Force supply chain risk. Accordingly, using the protocol in Appendix A, we interviewed DLA personnel at the Defense Supply Center in Richmond, Virginia, as well as at DLA headquarters.

We also interviewed representatives of high-technology companies known for their innovative supply chain risk management practices to learn more about their SCRM organizations, practices, and resources. Our protocol for these interviews is in Appendix C.

Finally, given that the Air Force might have its greatest leverage to address supply chain risk problems during the acquisition process, we interviewed personnel who work on acquisition of six weapon systems. Our protocol for these interviews is in Appendix D.

In Chapter 2, we present further background on supply chain risk management and on recent trends that have affected them. In Chapter 3, we summarize our review of literature and interviews with selected high-technology firms on current SCRM practices and outline a process for supply chain risk management. In Chapter 4, we examine existing DoD and Air Force guidance on managing supply chain risk and compare it to commercial best practices, with special attention to gaps between commercial best practices and DoD and Air Force guidance. In Chapter 5, we summarize our interviews with acquisition and sustainment personnel regarding Air Force supply chain risk management practices. In Chapter 6, we present the elements of prototype maps the Air Force may wish to consider developing for identifying and managing supply chain risks. In Chapter 7, we summarize our findings and present recommendations for the Air Force to improve its supply chain risk management.

---

[5] After this study was completed, the Air Force Material Command (AFMC) was reorganized and commodity councils were renamed commodity groups overseen by the 448 Supply Chain Management Wing (SCMW) Commodity Council (Kempf, 2012). Commodity Council (now Group) representatives we interviewed included those of the Landing Gear Commodity Council at the Ogden (Utah) Air Logistics Center (now Complex), the Communications and Electronics Commodity Council at the Warner Robins (Georgia) Air Logistics Center (now Complex), and the Propulsion, Instruments, and Accessories Commodity Council at the Oklahoma City (Oklahoma) Air Logistics Center (now Complex).

2. Background on Supply Chain Risk Management

There is no single authoritative definition of supply chain risk management. Nevertheless, definitions of supply chain, risk, and risk management can help in defining the term for our purposes.

In this chapter, we review definitions of supply chain risk, points at which industry and DoD consider it, dimensions they may consider, and how perceptions of risk may vary.

Defining and Measuring Risk

Enslow (2008, p. 3) describes the supply chain as including "all processes involved in making, moving, storing, or servicing physical goods . . . from raw material producers through to the end customer," including activities such as manufacturing, purchasing, warehousing, transportation, and inventory management done by an enterprise or on its behalf by suppliers, logistics providers, or service organizations. The International Organization for Standardization (ISO, 2009, p. 1), in turn, defines risk as the "effect of uncertainty on objectives." Applying the ISO definition of risk to a supply chain would yield a definition of supply chain risk as the effect on its objectives of uncertainty at any point in the end-to-end supply chain. Uncertainty, in turn, can lead to disruptions in the supply chain.

Further applying the ISO (2009, p. 2) definition of risk management—"coordinated activities to direct and control an organization with regard to risk"—to a supply chain would yield a definition of supply chain risk management as the coordination of activities to direct and control an enterprise's end-to-end supply chain with regard to supply chain risks. ISO (2009, p. 2) further defines a risk management framework as the "set of components that provide the foundations and organizational arrangements for designing, implementing, monitoring, reviewing, and continually improving risk management throughout the organization."[6]

---

[6] Readers may also be interested in the definition of supply chain management offered by the Council of Supply Chain Management Professionals (undated): "Supply chain management encompasses the planning and management of all activities involved in sourcing and procurement, conversion, and all logistics management activities. Importantly, it also includes coordination and collaboration with channel partners, which can be suppliers, intermediaries, third party service providers, and customers. In essence, supply chain management integrates supply and demand management within and across companies."

The term "supply chain management" can have different meanings in the commercial sector and within DoD. This difference can lead to different emphases for efforts to mitigate supply chain risks at different points in time. Industry typically applies the term to products that enterprises make, whereas DoD often applies it to products that it buys, particularly weapon systems (i.e., largely after they are made). As a result, industry considers the supply chain from product design through production to aftermarket support, ending with product disposal. DoD typically considers the supply chain during the weapon system acquisition process as it affects delivery and during the sustainment phase as it affects use, but not during the design phase. During production phases, DoD typically leaves supply chain risk management to its prime contractors—even these can still have profound effects on DoD operations, not only during production but, as we will discuss, in later support of weapon systems. Table 2.1 summarizes the differences between industry and DoD in managing supply chain risks.

During design and production, weapon system cost, performance, and schedule tend to dominate DoD considerations. The one exception is cybersecurity initiatives, a topic we will discuss below, where supply chain risk management starts in the design phase and includes selection of trusted upstream suppliers and assuring that hardware and software are free of malicious content (Lynn, 2010).

Regardless of how supply chain risk is considered, there are three dimensions for measuring its magnitude, as Figure 2.1 illustrates. These dimensions are

Table 2.1. Key Differences in When Industry and DoD Use the Term "Supply Chain Management"

Industry → Product	DoD → Weapon System
Design—supply chain management typically starts here	Acquisition — Design
Production — Supply chain — Assembly	— Manufacturing Original equipment manufacturer (OEM) and its suppliers
Aftermarket support — Supply chain	Sustainment—supply chain management typically starts here[a] — Supply chain

[a] Except cybersecurity initiatives, for which supply chain management typically starts in design.

Wieland and Wallenburg (2012) also discuss supply chain risk management as a way to help supply chain managers "cope with vulnerabilities both proactively by supporting robustness and reactively by supporting agility."

6

- The *likelihood* or probability of occurrence of an event that could cause adverse effects (i.e., produce harm or loss): As ISO (2009, p. 2) notes, "Risk is often expressed in terms of a combination of the consequences of an event (including changes in circumstances) and the associated likelihood of occurrence."
- The *expected consequence*, that is, what would happen to an enterprise should a risk occur: As ISO (2009, p. 2) notes, "Risk is often characterized by reference to potential events and consequences, or a combination of these." An example of harm or loss of low consequence resulting from a risk would be short delays in fulfillment of customer orders. An example of high consequence would be the release of a highly toxic substance that would harm or kill many individuals or any that could lead to the demise of the enterprise altogether. Consequence may include physical loss (e.g., of a production facility) or capacity loss (e.g., of ability to produce). An enterprise may mitigate consequence by replacing capacity even before its facility is replaced if it has or can access capacity elsewhere.

Figure 2.1. Three Dimensions of Risk

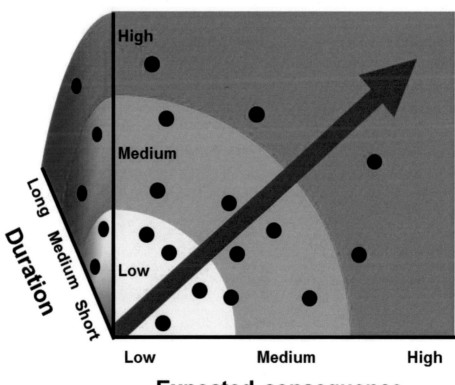

SOURCE: Adapted from Favre and McCreary (2008).

- The *duration*, that is, how long the risk event causes loss or harm to an enterprise: A short event, such as a power outage lasting less than an hour, is likely to have little lasting effect on an enterprise. A more significant event, requiring more than a year to replace facilities, equipment, or personnel, would obviously have a longer-lasting effect. The longer the duration of the consequence, the greater the harm or loss to an enterprise. If a risk cannot be avoided, then enterprises need to focus on reducing its duration or consequences so as to reduce total harm or losses.

Trends Affecting Supply Chain Risks

Just as the Air Force faces many of the same supply chain challenges as commercial enterprises do, so, too, have trends shaping commercial supply chains affected those for the Air Force.

Two major commercial trends that DoD and the Air Force have been adopting— inventory reductions and outsourcing[7]—can make supply chains more productive but also riskier. High inventory levels can buffer an organization against internal and external supply disruptions (although they also pose their own risks, as we will discuss). Minimal inventory levels resulting from "lean" and other initiatives provide no such buffer.

Similarly, internal production gives an enterprise control over the use and scheduling of its production assets. Outsourced production may require that an enterprise share production assets with other customers of the supplier. That is, an enterprise purchasing inputs from a supplier effectively shares that supplier's facilities with others purchasing the same or similar inputs from that same supplier. This reduces the enterprise's control over use and scheduling of assets, whereas an enterprise undertaking internal production for an input would have total control over the assets needed to produce it; those purchasing from a supplier would not. Consequently, outsourcing assembly, manufacturing, or production inputs may increase disruptions, particularly when

---

[7] Regarding outsourcing, we note that the Federal Activities Inventory Reform Act of 1998 (Public Law 105-270) directs that federal executive agencies, including DoD, submit to OMB by June 30 inventories of activities that are "inherently governmental" and commercial activities (i.e., activities that are not "inherently governmental") performed by federal employees every year. Activities identified as commercial may be competed against private-sector bidders using OMB Circular A-76, *Revised Supplemental Handbook*. If a private-sector bid is deemed cheaper, the activity is outsourced. In August 2001, President George W. Bush announced the President's Management Agenda, which included competitive sourcing as one of five initiatives to enhance government's effectiveness (OMB, 2001). In March 2009, Congress prohibited the initiation of any new public-private A-76 competitions (Public Law 111-8, the FY 2009 Omnibus Appropriations Act). In addition, the Obama administration issued a memo in 2009 calling for a review of existing contracts and giving guidance clarifying when government outsourcing of services is and is not appropriate (White House, 2009). Subsequent efforts by Congress to put a moratorium on insourcing (e.g., H.R. 1540, the National Defense Authorization Act) did not make it into law.

inventory buffers have been reduced, because the enterprise may have both less control and less visibility over external sources than it would for internal ones.

Other commercial-sector trends being adopted in DoD and the Air Force affecting their supply chain risks include supply base rationalization, which can lead to single or sole sourcing (Duffy, 2005); industry consolidations, which can similarly lead to less competition or fewer choices (Deans, Kroeger, and Zeisel, 2002); globalization (World Trade Organization, 2008), and virtual integration, or the blurring of the traditional boundaries between supply chain partners through the use of technology and information (Magretta, 1998). We discuss each of these below.

To reduce costs and improve supplier performance, many enterprises have analyzed their spending and supplier performance and rationalized their supply base. This often leads to a significant reduction in the number of suppliers. In response to a 2005 Office of Management and Budget memorandum (Johnson, 2005) that calls for "leveraging spending to the maximum extent possible," DoD and the Air Force have been analyzing their contracts, spending, and supplier performance, often through strategic sourcing initiatives that have led to the use of fewer suppliers. This creates a cost/risk trade-off. Using fewer suppliers can both decrease costs and increase supply risks because a larger percentage of inputs will be affected by a single supplier's performance. However, firms may also be able to work closely with those fewer suppliers to reduce theirs risks. On the other hand, working with multiple suppliers can limit the risks of a disruption from any one supplier, but it also limits how well firms can leverage their spending or work with suppliers to reduce their risks and improve performance.

Over time, as industries mature, they tend to consolidate as a result of mergers, acquisitions, and bankruptcies (Deans, Kroeger, Zeisel, 2002). In the early 1990s, DoD leaders became concerned that excess capacity in defense firms, resulting from a sharp decrease in defense spending from its Cold War peak in 1985, would lead to higher weapon system costs (Office of the Under Secretary of Defense, Comptroller, 2012). Consequently, DoD actively encouraged defense industry consolidation through mergers, acquisitions, and restructuring (Perry, 1996). These efforts resulted in "a dramatic decline in prime contractors in 10 of the 12 markets DoD identified as important to national security" (General Accounting Office, 1998, p. 2). This decline raised concerns about preserving competition with fewer choices for defense aerospace products and suppliers. Such reductions in the number of suppliers could, as noted, help leverage spending and reduce some risks of disruptions but increase others.

Another trend affecting supply chain risk is globalization. Seeking to lower total costs, broaden their customer base, and diversify risks, many enterprises have actively sought suppliers in low-cost countries, moved production there, and expanded marketing and sales beyond their traditional markets. These actions have led to longer and more

9

complex supply chains as products are customized to local markets and move through varying political, cultural, economic, and geographic environments as well as multiple distribution channels and transportation modes. Even given statutory requirements for supporting American industry, such trends have affected DoD (Hamre, 1998). As DoD moves away from its traditional defense industrial base, it will be tapping into the supply chains of enterprises that are often more global in nature.

The traditional lines between supply chain partners have also been blurring through virtual integration—the use of technology such as e-commerce to exchange information throughout the end-to-end supply chain (Magretta, 1998). Activities that enterprises used to do internally, such as ordering, configuring, and delivery, are now being done by customers, suppliers, or logistics providers. Enterprises are also developing multiple channels for serving customers. This makes tracking and managing supply chains, and risks to them, more complex. Such complexity requires sophisticated information systems for operations, management, and information sharing, which adds new costs and introduces additional risks to supply chains while managing others.

Last, buyer and societal concerns regarding environmental, fair labor, health and safety, and financial issues throughout the end-to-end supply chain broaden requirements for risk management beyond traditional categories. Such issues can cause dramatic changes in customer demand or even boycotts in the commercial sector, particularly in response to negative announcements. Changes in policies in government as well as political pressures regarding supplier selection can also create new supply chain risks.

Cybersecurity provides an excellent example of how major supply chain trends have increased DoD risks. Virtual integration of air, land, sea, and coalition forces and support, which reduces total costs and improves communications, has made warfighters increasingly reliant on information-communication technology (ICT). Increased outsourcing in the commercial sector, which manufactures DoD ICT, has increased the complexity and decreased the visibility of upstream suppliers of key ICT inputs. Globalization of the ICT supply chain has increased exposure to non-U.S.–based ICT suppliers, particularly in the less-visible upstream supply chain. The Defense Science Board Task Force on Mission Impact of Foreign Influence to DoD Software observed that "The software industry has become increasingly and irrevocably global" (Office of the Under Secretary of Defense for Acquisition, Technology, and Logistics, 2007). Indeed, a number of major attacks on critical U.S. ICT infrastructure led to adoption of the Comprehensive Cybersecurity Initiative. This included a global SCRM strategy, which we discuss below, as part of its implementation plan.

Traditional Approaches to Supply Chain Risks

Traditional approaches to supply chain risks were to buffer them with multiple suppliers, extensive frequent competition to assess market alternatives and try to lower purchase prices, expediting, increased order quantities, and maintaining inventory safety stocks and other stocks throughout the end-to-end supply chain (Giunipero and Eltantawy, 2004). Nevertheless, these buffering strategies also have risks and costs associated with them, including limited price leverage; increased variance in supply orders, quality, and delivery; exposure to each supplier's risks; limited opportunities for collaboration and continuous improvement; and having too much, too little, or obsolescent inventory (Table 2.2). All of these can lead to increased total costs. Inventory buffer stocks throughout the supply chain can also hide problems that enterprises should fix (Cordon, 1995).

Overall, the benefits realized in lower total costs and improved quality, delivery, and reliability from new supply chain management practices, although carrying new and different risks, increase the importance of shifting from reactive supply chain risk buffering to proactively identifying, understanding, and effectively managing end-to-end supply chain risks and vulnerabilities (Zsidisin, Ragatz, and Melnyk, 2003). Enterprises need to identify prospective risks and vulnerabilities that could affect the end-to-end supply chain, determine their probability, and assess the likely consequence of such events. Once prospective risks are identified, enterprises need to prioritize them; develop ways to avoid, prevent, or mitigate the most harmful ones; and develop execution plans to reduce the duration and consequences of those that might occur (Steele and Court, 1996;

Table 2.2. Traditional Supply Risk Buffering Strategies Also Have Risks

Strategy	Risks
Multiple sources of supply	Limits price leverage and increases variance in quality and delivery, exposes firms to each supplier's risks
Frequent and extensive competition	Limits opportunities for collaboration and continuous improvement
Expediting	Increases total costs
Increased order quantities	Increases bullwhip effect, which can amplify demand as orders move up the supply chain[a]
Inventory safety stocks	Increases total costs, obsolescence
Well-stocked supply pipeline	Increases total costs and hides supply chain problems

[a] The bullwhip effect refers to the amplification of a small perturbation in the downstream supply chain, such as a change in demand, as it moves up the supply chain. For more on the bullwhip effect in supply chains, see Lee, Padmanabhan, and Whang (1997).

LCP Consulting in conjunction with the Centre for Logistics and Supply Chain Management, 2003; and Zsidisin, Ragatz, and Melnyk, 2005).

Perceptions of Risks

Perception of what constitutes a risk and of the severity of risks varies across and within organizations. This is somewhat evident in recent surveys of risks managers (i.e., persons responsible for assessing and managing supply chain risks) and supply chain managers (Enslow, 2008; Hillman and Keltz, 2007). The surveys are not strictly comparable, given that only four areas of risk—supplier delays, logistics delays, natural disasters, and intellectual property theft—were addressed in both surveys. Nevertheless, the surveys offer some insight on the issues each group must address, and the priority they give to them.

Risks reported as of concern to risk managers[8] included

- price, including variability in raw-materials costs, cited by 55 percent
- supplier delays, quality, and disruptions, cited by 51 percent; these may be the result of supplier shortages; constraints in labor, equipment, facilities, or inputs; variable quality of inputs; or other causes such as fires, explosions, structural failures, hazardous spills, financial problems, or labor strife
- internal operations or infrastructure problems, cited by 41 percent; these risks may result from facility, labor, or equipment shortages or unavailability, as well as mechanical breakdowns, all of which may also be related to poor planning or management
- logistics delays or disruptions, including events that delay, disrupt, or affect the safety and security of road, rail, air, or ocean movements of inputs to and outputs from production, cited by 40 percent
- natural disasters, including earthquakes, floods, hurricanes, tornados, tsunamis, and volcanic eruptions, cited by 40 percent
- demand volatility leading to surges or shortfalls in production, repair, or distribution, cited by 36 percent
- brand reputation, including risks to reputation posed by recalls or labor strife, cited by 29 percent
- intellectual property theft, counterfeiting, or "gray market" distribution of products through unauthorized, unintended, or unofficial channels, cited by 26 percent; such risks may be posed by internal employees or supply chain partners

---

[8] Enslow (2008) surveyed, in cooperation with *Risk & Insurance* magazine, 110 risk managers located primarily in North America. Fifty-one percent of respondents were from large enterprises (with at least $1 billion in annual revenue), 30 percent were from midsize enterprises (with $50 million to $1 billion in annual revenue), and 19 percent were from small enterprises (with less than $50 million in annual revenue). Enslow did not provide a response rate for the survey.

or by the substitution of deceitful imitator products for key inputs to production or even final products.

Risks reported as of concern to supply chain managers[9] included

- supplier delays, quality, and disruptions, cited by 51 percent
- strategic risk, cited by 17 percent; strategic risks may include market conditions, financial stability, or the ability to successfully launch a new product or sell the right product in the right market; they are particularly challenging when demand and supply are highly variable and products have short life cycles
- natural disasters, cited by 15 percent
- geopolitical events, such as currency fluctuations, political unrest, and changes in trade policies, cited by 11 percent
- regulatory risks, including changes in taxes, customs, tariffs, and other restrictions on imports and exports, cited by 11 percent
- logistics delays or disruptions, cited by 10 percent
- other risks not explicitly queried, cited by 1 percent.

Figure 2.2, based on a survey of supply chain managers in eight industries, illustrates some supply chain risk concerns by industry. Not surprisingly, concerns about supply chain risks vary by industry.

Of these industries, "high-tech" and "aero and defense" are perhaps most relevant to the Air Force. In both industries, both "supplier failure" and "strategic risk" such as loss of manufacturing capacity or overreliance on one supplier are among the greatest concerns. Other risks of great concern among aerospace and defense supply chain managers but of less concern to those in "high-tech" industries include geopolitical events, regulatory risks, and logistics failures. Supply chain managers in the aerospace and defense industries reported that natural disaster risks are not applicable to them. We discuss below what may be driving this lack of concern.

When we compare the results of the survey of supply chain managers by industry (shown in Figure 2.2) to the results of the surveys of supply chain and risk managers noted above (Hillman and Keltz, 2007; Enslow, 2008), we see that there are differences even within the same functional area across industries. Therefore, should an enterprise rely on another to perform risk mitigation, it must understand possible differences in the perception of risk by enterprise or industry.

---

[9] Hillman and Keltz (2007) surveyed 89 supply chain managers who evaluated SCRM technology and services purchases at U.S. manufacturing and retail companies. Among respondents, 52 percent were from discrete manufacturing, 36 percent from process managing, and the remainder from retail, with 40 percent of respondents at firms with at least 15,000 employees and 33 percent at firms with fewer than 5,000 employees. Hillman and Keltz did not provide a response rate for their survey.

Figure 2.2. Supply Chain Risk Concerns Vary by Industry

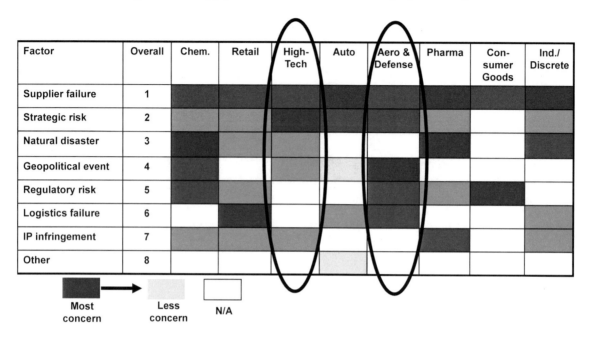

SOURCE: Hillman and Keltz (2007).

Although there are differences in perceptions of risk by industry or organization, several common practices to address risk have evolved over time. In the next chapter, we discuss evolving commercial practices in supply chain risk management.

3. Evolving Commercial Practices in Supply Chain Risk Management

Supply chain risk management is an evolving field. It poses myriad challenges, to which enterprises and researchers have taken a large number of different approaches over time.

In this chapter, we review the growing experience that leading enterprises have had with managing supply chain risks over time. From these, we derive a composite nine-step process for managing supply chain risks. We then assess how enterprises organize and staff supply chain risk management.

Overall, this chapter serves as a primer on evolving practices in supply chain risk management and as a reference for our subsequent discussions of how the Air Force and DoD might organize supply chain risk management. It focuses on corporate examples, but in some places it discusses DoD examples as well. Supply chain risk management is applicable to DoD enterprises and private enterprises equally, but, because it is more advanced in some private enterprises, our examples in this chapter tend to focus on the private sector.

Readers well versed in supply chain risk management may wish to skim before reviewing our more DoD-specific discussions, but those less familiar with the topic may find this a helpful introduction.

Growing Concerns with Supply Chain Risk Management

Supply chain risk management is challenging for several reasons. Often, risk mitigation strategies are costly, may involve procuring backup systems, or may involve establishing alternative sources of supply. The return on investment from mitigation strategies may be difficult to quantify and justify to management, and this may be especially true for investments to mitigate risks with large effects but low likelihood. Business environments are very dynamic, and an inventory of the risks that cause concern will change as the business environment evolves, new competitors and suppliers enter or leave the market, or governments and regulations change. There may be limited visibility of upstream supply risks, making it difficult to assess and communicate the exposure to risks to upper management. SCRM requires balancing and communicating the uncertainty that an event will happen, the costs of preparing for the event, and the costs of paying for the consequences.

Nevertheless, several recent events illustrate the constant presence of risks and the great consequences they have. Table 3.1 summarizes these events by category and their consequence to the supply chain. These events show that low-probability, high-consequence events may be difficult to predict but, when considered together, happen more often than might be suspected.

Among these events are natural disasters, such as hurricanes Katrina (August 2005), Rita (September 2005), and Ike (September 2008), which devastated several regions of the United States, including oil production facilities (and, as we will discuss below, threatened some Air Force suppliers); the 2008 earthquake in Chengdu, China, which killed more than 80,000 people and disrupted manufacturing there;[10] and the March 2011 earthquake and tsunami in Japan, which also killed hundreds of thousands and caused supply disruptions that reverberated throughout the global supply chain. Floods in Thailand in 2011 also shut down production of key electronic and automotive parts for many months. Even events such as the volcanic eruption in Iceland, which are peripherally connected to the global supply network, can also create disruptions that require management attention.

Other types of risks, such as labor unrest and changes in laws or regulations, have also occurred within the past decade. A ten-day West Coast port lockout in the early fall of 2002 led to shipping backlogs of more than 100 days. These backlogs took almost two

Table 3.1. Some Recent Events Illustrating the Importance of Proactive Risk Management

Risk Category	Event	Consequence to Supply Chain
Act of nature	Hurricanes	Production facilities, transportation routes, and employee homes heavily damaged
	Earthquakes/tsunamis	Capacities of high-tech and automotive industries reduced
	Volcanic eruptions	Flight cancellations
	Floods	Capacities of high-tech and automotive industries reduced
Labor unrest	Chinese factory riots West Coast port lockout	Plant shutdowns, distribution backlogs
Terrorist attack	September 11, 2001, terrorist attacks against the United States	Border and air traffic shut down

[10] The Chengdu earthquake illustrates not only how natural disasters can disrupt operations but how risk management efforts taken beforehand can help mitigate their effects. Because they have robust business continuity and SCRM plans, both Cisco and Intel, who had suppliers in Chengdu, were able to quickly assess the situation and smoothly transfer operations to other sources (Smith, 2008; Solomon and McMorrow, 2008).

16

months to clear and are estimated to have cost the U.S. economy $1 billion to $2 billion per day (Isidore, 2002; McKenna, 2007; and Hannon, 2008). Such events caused many enterprises with lean supply chains to realize that they needed to improve their risk management practices.

Finally, the September 11, 2001, terrorist attacks on the United States led to a shutdown of U.S. borders for days and grounding of nearly all flights both within and to and from the United States. Federal legislation has also prompted concerns with business disruption and continuity planning. The Sarbanes-Oxley Act of 2002 "mandates that organizations . . . understand the risks that may impact their financial reporting processes and requires them to put in place the proper controls" (Berman, 2004), that is, management processes and practices to manage risks that may affect financial performance of the enterprise. Although Sarbanes-Oxley does not specifically address business-continuity planning, complying with it requires that companies establish controls, engage in risk assessment, implement control activities, create effective communication and information flows, and monitor their control processes. This has led many enterprises to establish or strengthen business-continuity plans and programs. Because outsourced processes (i.e., the performance of external supply chain partners) can have a direct effect on an enterprise's financial statements, those that report to the U.S. Securities and Exchange Commission are required to assess the effectiveness of their suppliers' internal control structures pertinent to their contractual agreements. Some enterprises are beginning to require that their suppliers develop and share their business-continuity plans. This has led to the establishment of SCRM organizations and their placement within business-continuity programs.

Surveys of risk managers and supply chain managers have found that they may not be well prepared for events that affect their supply chains. In a survey of risk managers (Enslow, 2008), most reported having no formal risk process or a process with low effectiveness, and virtually none reported having a highly effective process. In a survey of supply chain managers, only about one in ten reported actively managing risk, and nearly half said they were concerned about risk but had no formal process for managing it (Hillman and Keltz, 2007). This is not surprising given the relatively recent awareness of increasing supply chain risks and establishment of business-continuity and SCRM organizations.

A lack of proactive supply chain risk management can delay recovery and increase the magnitude of the consequences of an event, as Figure 3.1 shows. The horizontal axis denotes elapsed time, and the vertical axis represents degree of change in the business or environment. The black line tracks how the business environment is changing, and the enterprise's reaction to that change is shown by the red line. Enterprises that are adept at

**Figure 3.1. Lack of Risk Management Can Delay Recovery and Increase
the Consequences and Duration**

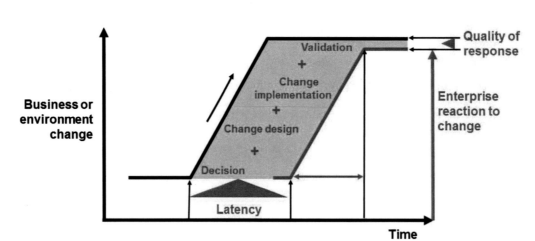

SOURCE: Adapted from Verstraete (2008).

adapting to change reduce latency, reducing the distance between the red and black lines.
When there are no plans for quickly identifying events that could affect an enterprise's
supply chain, there can be a delay in recognizing such events (decision latency). Once an
event has been recognized, if there are no plans for managing or mitigating the specific
type of event that has occurred, response delays (change design latency) will increase
while an enterprise determines the best response. Once a response has been designed, it
needs to be implemented, which further delays an enterprise's response (change
implementation latency). Finally, after implementation, an enterprise needs to determine
whether its response to the supply chain disruption was effective (validation latency). If
not effective, the implementation may need to be modified, further delaying the
enterprise's return to normal operations.

A well-publicized example of the costs of delay in responding to a supply chain
disruption was a brief fire caused by lightning at a Phillips Electronics semiconductor
plant in Albuquerque, New Mexico (Latour, 2001). The fire adversely affected the supply
of critical computer chips for both Nokia and Ericsson cell phones. Nokia noticed a
problem with its chip supply before Phillips notified it of the fire. As soon as it realized
that chip production would not be resumed quickly, Nokia "redesigned chips on the fly,
sped up a project to boost production, and flexed the company's muscle to squeeze more
out of other suppliers" (Latour, 2001). Ericsson did not have other chip suppliers and was
slow to react, failing to find alternative sources of supply. As a result of its ability to
detect the problem faster than Ericsson and execute a response, Nokia gained market
share at the expense of Ericsson. Ericsson eventually developed a proactive SCRM
approach, but too late to prevent the large losses associated with the fire in the Phillips

18

plant, as well as its exit from cell phone handset production (Norrman and Jansson, 2004).

Characteristics of Proactive Supply Risk Management

Proactive supply chain risk management requires an organization that develops guidance and policies for identifying and managing supply chain risks. This organization must develop the capability to target critical risks and to develop and execute risk management plans.

Proactive supply chain risk management also requires that an enterprise have a supply chain risk assessment and management process. Often supporting the process are tools such as risk maps for identifying, assessing, and monitoring supply chain risk, as well as strategies for mitigating and managing many supply chain disruptions. Strategies may include identifying or developing a second source or site for manufacture, holding inventory to cover requirements for the duration of the disruption, and, in the long term, designing future products and selecting suppliers to reduce overall supply chain risks.

The enterprises most successful at supply chain risk management have a formal SCRM program (Enslow, 2008). They create a partnership of corporate risk managers and supply chain operations. The risk manager mobilizes the enterprise against supply chain risks, and supply chain operations work to ensure that risk processes are designed cross-functionally and end-to-end and embedded into current activities. For example, cross-functional SCRM might include representatives from procurement, manufacturing, and sales. An end-to-end perspective would identify supply chain risk along all the points of the supply chain, including subtier suppliers.

We asked representatives from three companies how they were organized for supply chain risk management. All reported that they had an enterprise-wide SCRM organization that develops policies, processes, tools, internal metrics (such as number of suppliers with business-continuity plans), and supplier time-to-recovery commitments. These centralized organizations also institutionalize reporting requirements for supply chain risk management, which can include regular reports to the enterprise's board of directors.

One company reported that strategic business units identify, assess, and prioritize supply chain risks for their products and services. The strategic business units also develop and implement specific risk management plans, request and review supplier business-continuity plans, and monitor and report supply chain risk to their unit and enterprise management.

Although the alignment is not ideal, DoD or Air Force readers may consider the Air Force to be an enterprise, the major commands to be strategic business units, and centers within the Air Force to be divisions within business units. As we discuss below, the Air

Force needs to approach supply chain risk management across its entire "enterprise" as well as within each of its "strategic business units."

Cisco Systems, Inc., provides an example of organizing across an enterprise for supply chain risk management. Cisco has an SCRM team that is part of its Customer Value Chain Management (CVCM) organization (Harrington and O'Connor, 2009). Within the CVCM organization, the SCRM team partners with Global Supplier Management, which is responsible for sourcing decisions and managing relationships; Product Operations, which is responsible for developing products from engineering innovations; and Global Manufacturing Operations, which is responsible for global manufacturing and logistics. The CVCM organization partners with Cisco engineers to assess the resiliency of new products. The CVCM organization also partners with Cisco's suppliers, manufacturing partners, and transportation and logistics providers to continuously manage supply chain risks.

The four key elements of Cisco's program are

- the Business Continuity Planning Program, which works closely with internal partners (managers of different Cisco products) and external partners (suppliers of parts or assemblies and products as well as logistics partners—which, in the DoD context, may include the Defense Logistics Agency and the U.S. Transportation Command) "to document recovery plans and times and drive resiliency standards"
- Crisis Management, which is responsible for continuous global monitoring of and response to disruptions
- Product Resiliency, which helps Cisco's business units address supply chain vulnerabilities during product design and prioritize risk mitigation strategies while reducing their costs
- Supply Chain Resiliency, which identifies points in the supply chain where time-to-recovery would be unacceptably high and develops resiliency plans for these points.

In developing SCRM organizations, enterprises may seek to develop or impart certain skills. A survey of risk managers (Enslow, 2008) indicates that among skills important for success are

- strong networking and orchestration, indicated by 79 percent of risk managers
- basic understanding of end-to-end supply chain process, indicated by 77 percent
- effective articulation to colleagues of how risk initiatives deliver short-term operational or financial improvement, indicated by 70 percent
- ability to "talk the language" of the chief executive officer, chief financial officer, and enterprise-wide audiences to gain support for initiatives, indicated by 66 percent
- ability to educate functional personnel on key risk areas and best practices, indicated by 63 percent

- adeptness at aggregating risks across functional silos and business units to monitor total enterprise risk, indicated by 63 percent.

Strong networking and orchestration skills are particularly important because supply chain risks cut across different functions within the enterprise as well as suppliers external to the enterprise. Although the goal of supply chain risk management is to prevent adverse consequences (e.g., additional costs, short- and long-term loss of business) to the enterprise, it is often hard to justify expending resources for SCRM initiatives to prevent loss. Therefore, articulating how risk initiatives deliver short-term operational or financial improvement is particularly important. Supply chain risk managers also must be able to communicate with corporate leaders and audiences on enterprise-wide benefits for SCRM initiatives.

Representatives of the companies we interviewed reported that supply chain risk managers need to be able to educate different functional personnel on key risk areas and best practices for managing those risks. They also need to be adept at aggregating risks across functional silos and enterprise business units to monitor total enterprise risk.

Representatives from one company we interviewed told us that they seek to hire persons knowledgeable in supply chain management, which they say is harder to teach and then train in SCRM.

Because supply chain risk management is an emerging practice, enterprises are still experimenting with the best incentives, metrics, and procedures for it. Nevertheless, there are several common practices, which we review below as part of a composite SCRM process.

A Composite Process for Managing Supply Chain Risk

After conducting interviews and reviewing relevant literature, we identified a composite, multistep, continuous process for supply chain risk management. Figure 3.2 outlines this process, which is based on five previously proposed methods for analyzing supply vulnerabilities described in the literature.[11]

---

[11] Yates and Stone (1992) suggest four elements for risk appraisal: existence, including awareness of the potential for possible loss; identity, including identification of specific losses that might occur; likelihood, including determination of the likelihood of a possible loss; and significance, including assessment of the significance of a possible loss.

Zsidisin, Ragatz, and Melnyk (2003) propose a second model based on awareness, prevention, remediation, and knowledge management. Awareness is both internal and external and may include financial reports, supply chain mapping, and use of audit instruments. Prevention includes identification, assessment, treatment, and monitoring of risks and may include such actions as a risk register. Remediation includes planning how to minimize the consequence and duration of a risk and the resources required to address it. Knowledge management includes tracking results and actions for continuous improvement.

Figure 3.2. Supply Chain Risk Management Is a Multistep, Continuous Process

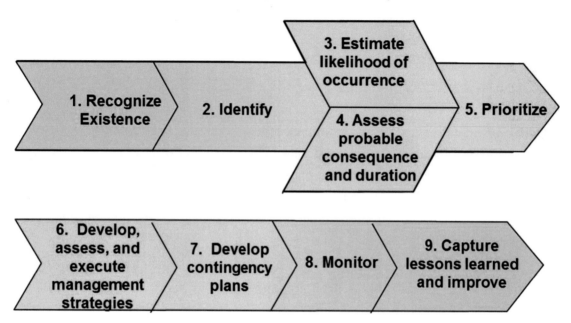

Next we define each step and provide additional details on steps to identify risks (step 2); prioritize risks (step 5); develop, assess, and execute a risk management strategy (step 6); and capture lessons learned to improve risk management (step 9).

Step 1: Recognize Existence of Risk

Before an enterprise can address supply risks, it must be aware that supply vulnerabilities exist (Zsidisin, Ragatz, and Melnyk, 2003). An enterprise must also be aware that its actions, or inaction, can create supply chain risks. The Air Force has

---

They also suggest a model adapted to the strategic-sourcing process. Its first step is to analyze internal requirements and understand risk tolerance. Its second step is to analyze the supply market to understand market risks. Its third step is to determine the approach to risk management and relationship types to reduce and buffer risks. Its fourth step is to identify and evaluate suppliers, including assessing the risks of each. Its fifth step is to build and manage relationships, including monitoring risks in them.

Ziegenbein and Nienhaus (2004) suggest a four-part continuous SCRM process. Its elements include identification of risks, including a structured documentation of risks and their sources; assessment of risks, including measuring their likelihood and consequence; controlling risks, including evaluating risks and deciding how to cope with them; and monitoring risks, including a transparent overview of supply chain risks at all times.

LCP Consulting in conjunction with the Centre for Logistics and Supply Chain Management (2003) proposed an SCRM flow beginning with a description of the supply chain. An enterprise may then use vulnerability self-assessment templates to document risks in such areas as demand, supply, environment contingency, process, and control. Once the self-assessment is complete, an enterprise may evaluate the implications of the risks it faces, including their scale, duration, recovery, and cost. An enterprise can then identify the actions it needs to take such as mitigation strategies or developing contingency plans for the risks with the greatest consequences to its operations.

undertaken this step through its sponsorship of research on identifying and managing risks associated with agile supply chains, as well as, in part, through its reorganization of the Air Force Materiel Command.

Step 2: Identify Risks

Enterprises need to identify the possible risks associated with a prospective supply strategy. An example of a supply chain risk may be disruptions caused by natural disasters. One way to visualize these risks, which are related to location, is to map them, as we illustrate below.

Other methods for identifying risks include brainstorming, interviews, workshops, supply chain mapping/description,[12] the Delphi Method,[13] fault or event tree analysis (Ziegenbein and Nienhaus, 2004),[14] and Nominal Group Technique (Zsidisin, Panelli, and Upton, 2000).[15] Some authors recommend assessing vulnerabilities by categories of external risks and internal risks (Peck et al., 2003).[16] Others (e.g., Steele and Court, 1996) recommend a less structured approach so as not to inhibit consideration of any risks.

Supplier participation is necessary for a vulnerability analysis (Steele and Court, 1996). Few organizations have the resources to eliminate all vulnerabilities (and those that do may need to employ them elsewhere). Hence, both customers and suppliers must work together to identify supply vulnerabilities, an essential step in risk management.

Step 3: Estimate the Likelihood of Occurrence

In this step, enterprises estimate the likelihood of occurrence of a prospective vulnerability. Some authors (e.g., Steele and Court, 1996) assign a relative weight to the

---

[12] Supply chain mapping identifies all members, facilities, linkages, and flows of goods, information, and money in the end-to-end supply chain from upstream raw materials suppliers through manufacture to downstream delivery to the final customer, use, and then disposal (Gardner and Cooper, 2003).

[13] The Delphi Method relies on a series of questionnaires given to a group of experts to discern a consensus and reasons for disagreement (Linstone and Turoff, 2002).

[14] Fault or event tree analysis breaks down a system risk event into component failures step by step by linking failure events with their causes. Because fault tree analysis is used for qualitative and quantitative analysis of systems, it is essential that for a risk, every cause be considered in the fault tree and, conversely, that every mentioned cause is actually needed to trigger the event (Schellhorn, Thums, and Reif, 2002, p. 1).

[15] Nominal Group Technique involves individuals first generating their own ideas, then sharing them with a group, before ranking each (Van De Ven and Delbecq, 1974).

[16] External risks may include demand, supply (e.g., supplier failure, interruption in inbound shipments), or environment (e.g., natural disasters, accidents, terrorism, sabotage, business conditions). Internal risks may include control, process, and contingency plans to mitigate and manage the effect of a risk. For a more complete list of risks by type, see Appendix B, which lists risks queried in our interviews.

probability of occurrence. Others (Ziegenbein and Nienhaus, 2004) classify the possibility of occurrence into categories such as unlikely, possible, likely, and very likely.

Step 4: Assess the Probable Consequences and Duration If Realized

In this step, concurrent with Step 3, the organization assesses the relative total consequence or significance of the prospective loss to calibrate the exposure of the business. The total consequence of a given risk is a function of its scale, scope, duration, recovery time, and total cost. A risk's total consequence to the enterprise can be ranked as low or high (Steele and Court, 1996) or as low, medium, significant, or fatal (Ziegenbein and Nienhaus, 2004).

Step 5: Prioritize Risks

Rather than addressing all vulnerable areas at once, enterprises may focus their SCRM efforts on those events where these efforts are likely to provide the greatest relief (Steele and Court, 1996). In this step, enterprises prioritize risks by their significance so as to focus resources available for eliminating, mitigating, and managing the most important risks.

Because each commodity, product, or service has a different risk profile (Giunipero and Eltantawy, 2004), and identifying, assessing, and planning for supply chain risks require considerable time and resources, enterprises need a way to prioritize SCRM efforts. One way to prioritize risks is to plot by total consequence and likelihood (Zsidisin, Ragatz, and Melnyk, 2003). This can help identify risks that are behind or beyond an acceptable risk frontier or risks that are acceptable to an enterprise and those that are unacceptable to it and must be managed. Figure 3.3 depicts this notional approach.

Enterprises may also choose to assign categories of likelihood, duration, and consequence to risks and then prioritize risks by these. Table 3.2 illustrates how Steele and Court (1996) prioritize supply risks for management action based on whether a risk

Figure 3.3. Plotting Risk Exposure to Better Understand It

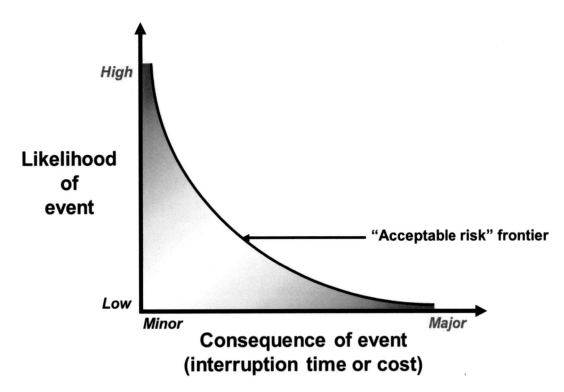

SOURCE: Adapted from Zsidisin, Ragatz, and Melnyk (2003).

Table 3.2. Steele and Court's Prioritization of Supply Risks

Priority	Likelihood	Duration	Consequence
1	High	Long	High
2	Medium	Long	High
3	High	Short	High
4	Medium	Short	High
5	High	Long	Low
6	Low	Long	High
7	Medium	Long	Low
8	Low	Short	High
9	Low	Long	Low
10	High	Short	Low
11	Medium	Short	Low
12	Low	Short	Low

SOURCE: Adapted from Steele and Court (1996).

has a high, medium, or low likelihood of occurrence, whether its duration would be short or long, and whether its consequence would be high or low.

Another way to prioritize and visualize risks is to map their likelihood and consequence into a risk matrix (Ziegenbein and Nienhaus, 2004). The Air Force has standardized a two-dimensional, five-by-five matrix for assessing risks during weapon system acquisition, as shown in Figure 3.4. This matrix establishes as A-Risk those risks

25

Figure 3.4. A Two-Dimensional Risk Matrix Can Help Prioritize SCRM Efforts

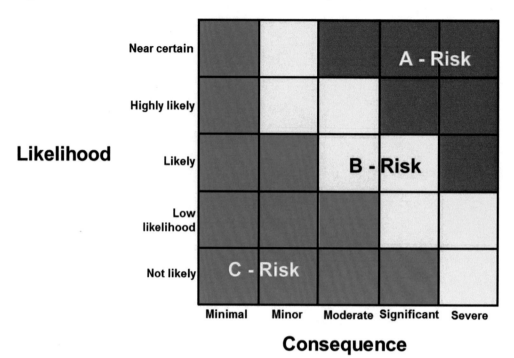

SOURCE: Payton (2008).

with the highest likelihood and severity, giving lower priority to C-Risk events, which have lesser consequence or probability of occurrence.

A recent Army Materiel Command Strategic Sourcing effort had key stakeholders review a list of prospective sustainment supply chain risks and rank them by importance.

Step 6: Develop, Execute, and Assess a Risk Management Strategy

This step of the SCRM process involves developing, assessing, and executing strategies to reduce the likelihood or mitigate the consequence or duration of prospective risks (Zsidisin, Ragatz, and Melnyk, 2003). For low-priority risks (i.e., those with low likelihood of occurrence and low total consequence), an enterprise may want to ignore or accept the risk. For high-priority risks (i.e., those with high likelihood of occurrence and high total consequence), an enterprise may try to avoid the loss occurrence altogether or accept and reduce its likelihood, consequence, or duration.[17] If the likelihood,

---

[17] To *avoid supplier disruptions*, enterprises can rigorously assess suppliers, carefully select them (using certification and prequalification), and frequently monitor or audit them for viability, quality (using statistical process control), reliability, and dependency (i.e., enterprises' percentage of supplier's total business). They can also establish multiple two-way communication channels for sharing forecasts and plans. They can gain or maintain visibility into the supplier's operations and require a quality management program and contingency plan. They can also align the supplier's incentives with their own, penalize poor

consequence, or duration of a risk cannot be reduced, then an enterprise needs to identify prospective operational or risk-sharing or transfer measures to mitigate the risk (Ziegenbein and Nienhaus, 2004).

Figure 3.5 illustrates how supply risk management strategies of enterprises may vary by level of planning (i.e., strategic or long term, tactical or medium term, and operational or short term) and strategy for dealing with risk. For example, a long-term strategy for avoiding or reducing supplier problems is to have a rigorous supplier selection process followed by regular audits of supplier facilities, processes, and finances. Another strategy to reduce supply risks is to have multiple sources, if feasible. A third long-term strategy is to share or transfer the risk by including penalties in contracts for unreliable supply. A short-term strategy is to monitor supplier delivery dates and quantities (as we noted Nokia did for its chip supply) to quickly detect emerging problems at suppliers. A medium-term strategy could be to maintain extra inventory or safety stock, but many enterprises prefer not to do this because of the added costs and risk of obsolescence or eventual disposal resulting from excess inventory.

Prospective actions, depending on probability of risk, consequence, and duration, can range from eliminating the need for a commodity to finding alternatives for it to taking no immediate action. Because some prospective risk prevention or mitigation efforts can be quite costly, enterprises need to evaluate each prospective strategy's costs and benefits. They should then gain management support and implement those strategies that are cost-effective (Kiser and Cantrell, 2006).[18]

---

performance (using fines or reduced business), reward good performance (using gain sharing, increased business, and supplier recognition), and share financial risks. Last, they can encourage joint improvement initiatives and direct access to knowledge workers.

To *prevent demand (volatility) risk*, enterprises can develop industry standards, common product "building blocks," or collaborative forecasting. *Process risk prevention* includes using ISO 9000 standards for process control, increasing supply chain visibility, and reducing lead times.

To *mitigate supplier risks*, enterprises can work with the supplier to improve its performance. They can also hold inventory (e.g., emergency supplies), obtain design specifications (i.e., technical data enabling them to develop supplier products internally or purchase them from another source), require that the supplier develop alternative sites, use dual or multiple sourcing, develop an alternative source, and move special tooling.

To *mitigate demand risk*, enterprises can hold safety stock inventory or develop multiple sources.

Process risk mitigation also includes holding safety stock inventory and using multiple sourcing.

To develop *contingency options to reduce supplier risks*, enterprises can establish a second source contract or identify and introduce alternative sources. Contingency options for *demand (volatility) risk* include identifying strategies to ration supply or reduce inventory and plans for their introduction. *Process risk contingency options* include identifying strategies to shift production or flow and plans for their execution.

[18] What an enterprise considers to be "cost-effective" will likely depend on its level of risk aversion and resources available to mitigate risks that may be seen as having low likelihoods but catastrophic consequences.

Figure 3.5. Example of Supply Risk Management

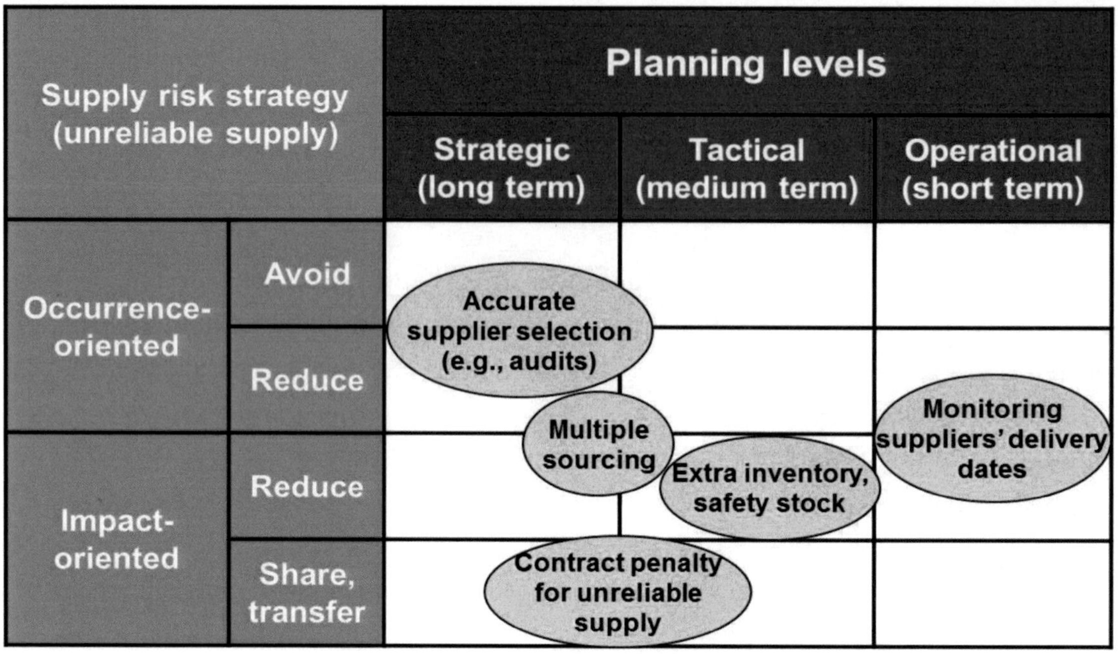

Supply risk strategy (unreliable supply)		Planning levels		
		Strategic (long term)	Tactical (medium term)	Operational (short term)
Occurrence-oriented	Avoid	Accurate supplier selection (e.g., audits)		
	Reduce			Monitoring suppliers' delivery dates
Impact-oriented	Reduce	Multiple sourcing	Extra inventory, safety stock	
	Share, transfer	Contract penalty for unreliable supply		

SOURCE: Ziegenbein and Nienhaus (2004).
NOTES: The terms "strategic," "tactical," and "operational" differ from the way the Air Force uses these terms. Here, "strategic" is long term, "tactical" is midterm, and "operational" is short term.

Figure 3.6 illustrates the different effects of two prevalent supply chain improvement strategies. The upper right quadrant indicates that a combination of outsourcing and reducing internal inventory buffers could reduce costs but increase the risk of supply chain disruptions, which in turn can reduce sales and revenue. The arrows point to potential risk mitigation strategies. The external strategy is to work with suppliers to improve responsiveness and reduce lead-time variability. The internal strategy is to increase inventory buffers. The lower right quadrant shows the trade-off of decreased risk of supply chain disruption at the cost of increased inventory and forgoing potential savings from outsourcing. Enterprises can mitigate the risk of holding inventory by improving the accuracy of demand forecasts, but this can be difficult to achieve, depending on the underlying causes of demand variability. Alternatively, enterprises can hold less inventory and improve the responsiveness of the supply chain to disruptions. This reduces the need for inventory and increases risk protection through risk transfer or insurance.

Figure 3.6. Example of Supply Risk Mitigation Strategies

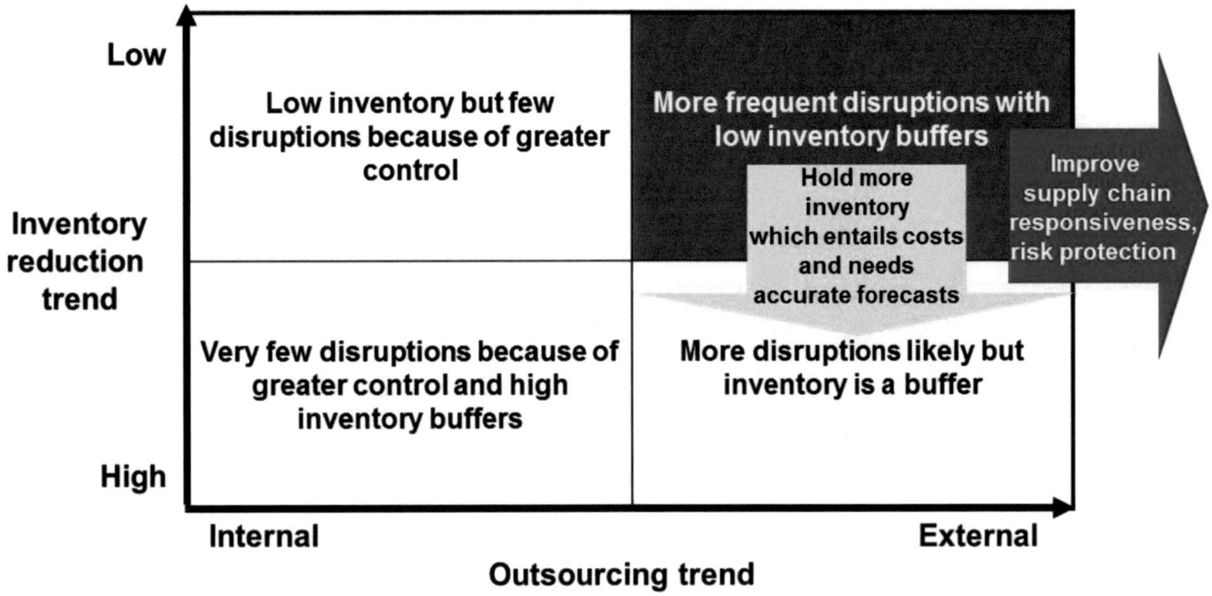

SOURCE: Adapted from Enslow (2008).

Step 7: Develop Contingency Plans

This step focuses on developing contingency plans for disruptions because not all risks can be effectively avoided, adequately mitigated, or even identified. Contingency plans can help enterprises respond to unforeseen disruptions quickly. These are detailed recovery or remediation plans for shortening the duration of a disruption, minimizing its consequences, and identifying the resources to execute the plan quickly (Zsidisin et al., 2003). As discussed above, the duration of a risk can be reduced by developing proactive risk management plans that reduce the decision latency to react to an event, reduce the reaction plan design latency, reduce the implementation latency, and reduce the execution time of a recovery plan.

Step 8: Monitor Continuously

After establishing a supply strategy and associated risk management plan, organizations should continuously monitor the environment for any change in prospective supply chain risks that warrant modification of the supply strategy or risk management plan (Zsidisin, Ragatz, and Melnyk, 2003). Such monitoring should be a broad-based responsibility of the customer or buyer, the supplier, other logistics partners, and other upstream and downstream elements in the supply chain.

29

Step 9: Capture Lessons Learned and Improve

This step focuses on continuous learning and knowledge management. When a supply disruption occurs, an enterprise needs to conduct postincident audits to determine the cause of the disruption and to document any lessons learned for better managing future events. The audits should also address any deficiencies identified in past risk assessments, mitigation strategies, and contingency plans (Zsidisin, Ragatz, and Melnyk, 2003).

Figure 3.7 summarizes how one company, Hewlett-Packard (HP), identifies the consequences and duration of differing risks on its supply chain management strategies (Verstraete, 2008). For example, a supplier's location, financial security, regulations, workforce practices, and quality can have a large effect on risks for HP's globalization and outsourcing strategy. Note particularly that natural and man-made hazards have a large effect when enterprises use sole sourcing, lean practices, or distribution hubs. Note further that the risks to quality are high when using globalization and outsourcing, sole sourcing, supply tiering (i.e., a multitier supply chain where many suppliers add value at different points along the supply chain), and returns management (also known as the reverse supply chain).

Figure 3.7. Example of How Hewlett-Packard Manages Risk

High impact / Moderate impact

Supply Chain Management Strategy	Risks: Natural/ man-made hazards	Country	Supplier bankruptcy	Network/soft-ware outage	Internet provider	Regulatory	Commodity price	Workforce practices	Logistics failure	Inventory	Quality
Globalization and outsourcing	Moderate	High		Moderate	High	High		High	Moderate		High
Sole sourcing	High	Moderate	High		High		Moderate	Moderate			High
Lean practices	High		Moderate	Moderate					High	High	Moderate
Distribution hubs	High			Moderate					High		
Commodity dependency	Moderate	Moderate					High		Moderate		
Demand visibility/ variability				Moderate			High			High	
Supply tiering	Moderate		High		Moderate	Moderate			Moderate		High
Returns management					Moderate	High			Moderate	Moderate	High

Exposure and risk to the bottom line are key criteria for ranking high impact areas

SOURCE: Adapted from Verstraete (2008).

How Enterprises Organize and Staff Supply Chain Risk Management

How do enterprises organize and staff their supply chain risk management organizations? Our research found that much effort to mitigate supply chain risks occurs early in a product life cycle. This is because strategies to mitigate risk can have greater consequences if implemented in the design stage rather than in the production and postproduction (i.e., sustainment) stages. Design decisions can affect the risks, such as proprietary designs or using a technology that is approaching obsolescence, throughout its life cycle. The effect is one of decreasing availability for SCRM strategies over the product life cycle, particularly if the life cycle from design to production to postproduction spans many years, and, most important, if the demand for production and service of a product and its component decreases (Chenoweth, Arkes, and Moore, 2010). Figure 3.8 notionally shows how demand for production or aftermarket services varies over the course of a product life cycle.

Addressing Supply Chain Risk During Design

Several SCRM strategies are available in the product design phase that are typically not available once production begins, including

Figure 3.8. Parts Demand During Product Life Cycle

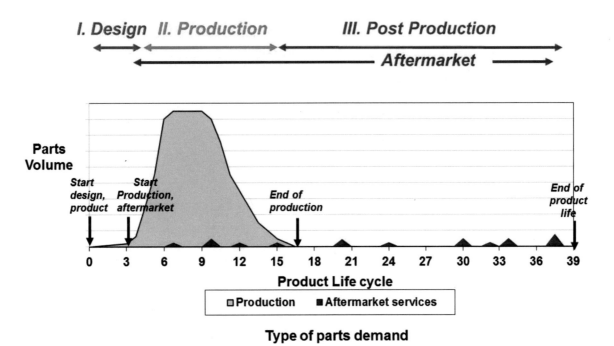

SOURCE: Adapted from Chenoweth, Arkes, and Moore (2010).

31

- involving supply chain personnel such as those in purchasing, manufacturing, and aftermarket support and key suppliers early in the product design phase to identify prospective supply chain risks and develop strategies to avoid or mitigate them
- monitoring and avoiding obsolescence in parts, technologies, and processes starting in the design phase and then throughout a product's life—a very important proactive strategy to reduce supply chain risks
- reducing the product's complexity by using standard parts as much as possible and by maximizing the commonality of parts across an enterprise's products; this strategy reduces the number of unique parts and increases the volume of demand, particularly in the postproduction phase when demand is likely to be much lower and more variable, which in turn can increase the risk of suppliers exiting the business
- involving suppliers in the design of systems, products, and parts
- negotiating with potential suppliers on the terms and conditions for the option to own technical rights of design should the buyer decide to exercise it; doing this in the design phase can help avoid problems of later having to deal with sole-source suppliers charging premium prices or providing poor support when the buyer no longer has other options.

Efforts during design and acquisition to reduce supply chain risks can involve many functions. Early involvement in the design process by marketing, supply chain managers, manufacturing, finance, and engineering can be essential to ensuring optimal supply chain performance.

Figure 3.9 illustrates the top-down, cross-functional approach to addressing supply chain issues during product design used by Samsung Data Systems. The measures of supply chain performance, listed on the right of the figure, include supply availability, lead time, and total cost. Total cost elements (shown in blue) include one-time product-specific investment, material cost, process cost (including manufacturing, assembly, and test), inventory cost, and transportation cost.

The process produces an estimate of supply chain performance based on inputs from the cross-functional team members. Typical inputs from marketing include projected demand for the product by region. Manufacturing provides estimates on throughput and manufacturing lead time. Supply chain team members provide strategies for distribution and component sourcing to meet the market and manufacturing demand. Engineering designs the product to meet form, function, and performance to include quality requirements.[19]

---

[19] HP has also successfully implemented design for supply chain concepts (Cargille and Fry, 2006). In a highly competitive printer market, HP management realized that even relatively small gains in efficiency could have a large effect on market share. By designing products to minimize the amount of packing material required, HP was able to increase shipping volumes without increasing shipping cost. Designing printers with built-in, multilanguage function allowed HP to use one basic design across multiple markets. When HP merged with Compaq Computer, it found that design differences in the server racks between HP

**Figure 3.9. Leading Companies Have Supply Chain Performance Goals
in Product Design**

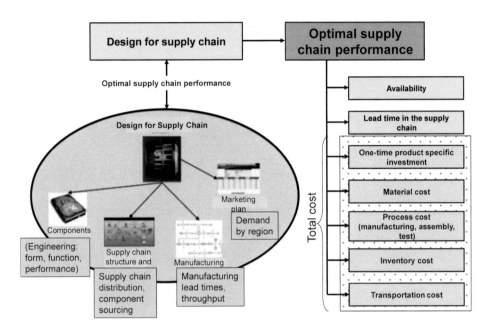

SOURCE: Samsung Data Systems (undated).

Design for supply chain in the Air Force context can be even more complex than it is for Samsung, but the general principles of the concept can still apply. The Air Force has an additional challenge because it is a consumer not the producer of weapon systems. Although the Air Force may want to use common parts across weapon systems, supplier relationships with multiple OEMs may make this difficult. HP recommends starting small and proving the concept before expanding to the entire organization. Similarly, the Air Force could strategically choose the parts that would be best candidates for design to reduce supply chain risks and work with OEMs to pilot the concept.

As Figure 3.10 shows, decisions made early in the weapon system design process can have continuing effects on life-cycle needs for a product and hence on its supply chain risks. The process begins with selection of a proprietary technology or part. Should a product proceed to the technology development phase while its technology is still immature, it can add costs and schedule delays as the supplier tries to improve

---

and Compaq required the ordering, stocking, and distributing of 12 different rail kits. By developing a common design, HP was able to reduce costs by $32 million dollars. At the same time, designers may often be taxed to meet tight deadlines and develop innovative products. Adding a requirement to consider supply chain implications of a design can be challenging.

33

Figure 3.10. Notional Example of How Decisions Early in the Acquisition Phase Can Increase Supply Chain Risks

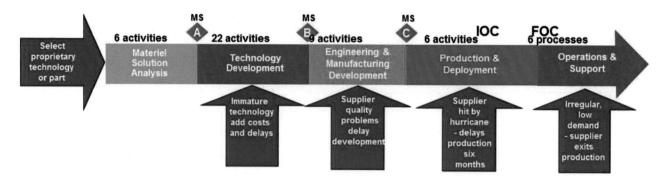

SOURCE: AFI 63-101 (2009).

performance to meet customer requirements. In the engineering and manufacturing development phase, any supplier quality problems will delay development. In the production and deployment phase, any disruptions to supplier production from natural disasters, such as floods, tornados, hurricanes, earthquakes, or fires, could significantly delay production. Last, in the operations and support phase, irregular or low demand can lead the supplier to halt production.

Several DoD space examples illustrate these problems.[20] One weapon system program saw its total costs grow and its schedule delayed because of a lack of specifications, third-tier subcontractor failures, and an inability to trace the sources of some components. Another program also experienced increased costs as a result of the need to redesign and retest key parts. These problems arose as a result of rework, replacement, and tests after failures of the parts that were mission-critical units.

Addressing Supply Chain Risk During Production

By the time the production phase begins, technologies, parts, assemblies, and suppliers have been selected and contracts signed. Although actions in the production phase may not have as great an effect on supply chain risks (e.g., life-cycle service) as those executed in the acquisition phase, leading enterprises still undertake several strategies to avoid, mitigate, or otherwise manage them. These include

- identifying remaining risk exposure and its effects on schedule and short- and long-term costs
- working with key suppliers to develop business-continuity plans and commit to an estimated time-to-recovery

---

[20] Personal communication with RAND colleague Mel Eisman, April 2010.

- working with key suppliers to reduce lead times and improve performance (e.g., quality, cost)
- encouraging "flow-down" to lower-tier suppliers of similar agreements and performance improvements
- ensuring supplier commitment to postproduction aftermarket services in the production contract
- negotiating potential access to technical data beforehand so as to assure supply in the event the supplier exits the business or attempts to exercise monopoly power over its proprietary technology.

Many of these enterprises such as Toyota assemble the final product themselves. For the Air Force to implement such practices, it would likely need to stipulate in its contract with the OEM that the OEM will assemble the weapon system and write contracts with suppliers to follow these practices.

Figure 3.11 illustrates how one enterprise, Cisco Systems, Inc., understands its production supply chain risks.[21] It lists sample disruptions with an estimate of their likely effect on revenue independent of whether the location is a supplier, contract manufacturer, or Cisco location. Cisco can make these estimates because it knows what products would be affected by a disruption at each location as well as the time it will take to recover.

Cisco identifies prospective events for each of its sites. Prospective events may include earthquakes, typhoons, and floods. Cisco considers both its own and supplier sites, including foundry and contract manufacturer (CM) sites, and particularly for single- or sole-sourced parts and for sites that are related to high revenue or critical products. Figure 3.12 illustrates how Cisco focuses its supply chain risk management on sites and possible events at each. Those at the top have the greatest total consequence to Cisco.

Cisco also ranks its product families and products by the revenue they generate. Figure 3.13 shows this ranking and how 25 product families and 100 products generate half the revenue for the firm. Cisco focuses its top SCRM efforts on products with the highest revenue generation. It devotes the most SCRM resources to these products and locations associated with their manufacture and distribution and fewer resources to products that generate lower revenue.

---

[21] Cisco had painful experiences with inadequate management of supply chain risks, particularly those posed by changes in economic conditions. In 2001, Cisco's inability to adjust to changing economic conditions led it to take a $2.1 billion inventory write-down, possibly the largest in history. See "The 11 Greatest Supply Chain Disasters" (2006) and Berinato (2001).

Figure 3.11. Example of Cisco Systems Understanding of Supply Chain Risk

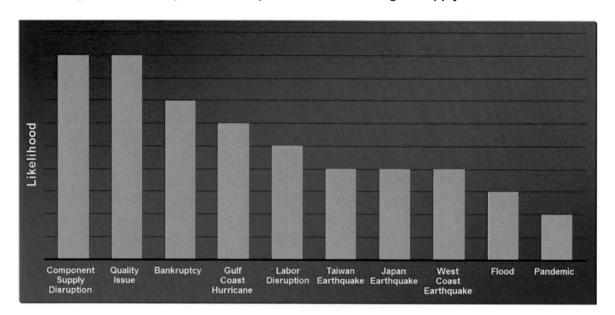

© 2007 Cisco Systems, Inc. All rights reserved.   **Used with permission**

Cisco Confidential

SOURCE: O'Connor (2008). Used with permission.

Cisco continuously monitors events throughout the world to quickly identify those that might adversely affect its supply chains. Figure 3.14 illustrates how Cisco manages its response to an event. Because it knows exactly where its suppliers' production facilities are located and what parts and products they support, when an event occurs Cisco can fairly quickly determine which suppliers, products, and customers may be affected and the effect on revenue. For example, when a 2008 earthquake struck Chengdu, Cisco, because of its previous mapping of supplier production locations and products, was able to identify the products and supply partners affected, and the likely time-to-recovery and effects on revenue. (Figure 3.14 shows the type of map and information Cisco would portray but not production and distribution locations, which are considered proprietary.) Because its suppliers have committed to a time-to-recovery in event of disaster, Cisco can also determine how long it might take suppliers to resume production at a facility and thus determine if it needs to execute a predetermined backup strategy such as shifting work to another location or supplier or drawing down emergency inventory. All of these actions reduce the time between supply chain disruption and resumption of normal operations, which in turn reduces the total consequence of an event.

Figure 3.12. Cisco Supply Chain Risk Management Is Event- and Location-Focused

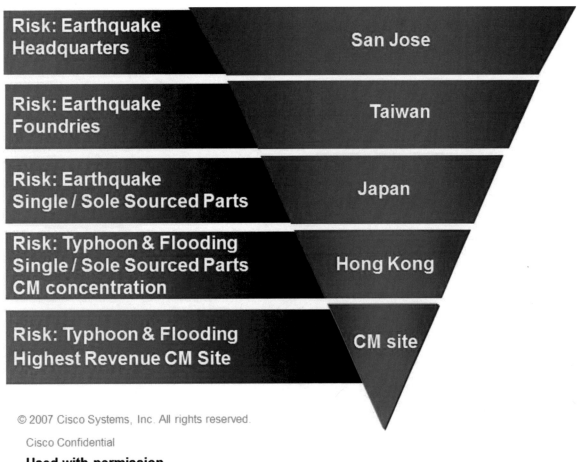

© 2007 Cisco Systems, Inc. All rights reserved.

Cisco Confidential

Used with permission

SOURCE: O'Connor (2008). Used with permission.

Altogether, the Cisco experience shows how enterprises, including the Air Force, may seek to address supply chain risks during production, even if production is outsourced. It also shows the variety of risks that supply chain risk managers must consider, and how they can identify supply chain risks that are important to them. Below, we will review how the Air Force considers supply chain risks and which tools such as risk maps similar to those Cisco uses it might develop to identify and manage them, particularly risks by location.

Addressing Supply Chain Risk After Production

Once production ceases, the only demands for product parts are those required for maintenance, repair, and replacement. Such demands tend to be lower, more variable, and more uncertain, especially over time, than those for production. Indeed, a specific part may not fail for years but then suddenly need to be replaced in all operating products. In

Figure 3.13. Cisco Supply Chain Risk Management Priorities Consider Product Revenue

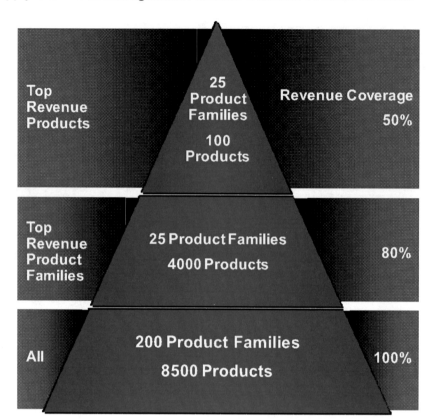

© 2007 Cisco Systems, Inc. All rights reserved.

SOURCE: O'Connor (2008). Used with permission.

the interim, that part supplier may have exited the business because there is little or no demand for it.

Consequently, SCRM strategies available after production tend to be quite different and more expensive and limited than those earlier in the product life cycle. If an agreement is not already in place to assure aftermarket support, one of the first SCRM strategies is to determine supplier availability for such support. Given the lower volume and higher variability, suppliers may need incentives to provide support. If there is no supplier, a customer may seek to develop one. Having access to technical information for parts no longer in production can facilitate finding a new source. If technical information is not available, a part may be reverse-engineered or a substitute developed. However, the cost of such efforts can be prohibitive for some parts.

Figure 3.14. Overview of Cisco Management Response to Chengdu Crisis

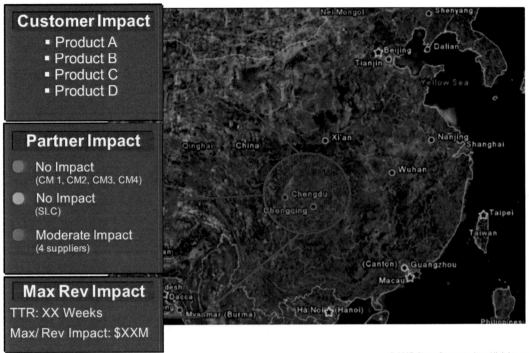

© 2007 Cisco Systems, Inc. All rights reserved.

SOURCE: O'Connor (2008). Used with permission.

Ideally, the Air Force should set up the terms and conditions for acquiring technical data for its parts upfront as it is acquiring a weapon system. An alternative SCRM strategy would be to purchase or retire whole products for parts. Still another strategy, should a supplier give notice of halting production, would be to buy an estimated lifetime supply of the parts. Some of these strategies may be expensive, especially if future demand is uncertain or will extend many years into the future, further increasing uncertainty.[22]

Summary of Emerging Practices

Our review found a number of emerging best SCRM practices. Leading firms begin thinking about short-term (i.e., production) and long-term (i.e., aftermarket) supply chain risk management as early as possible in the product design process to avoid or mitigate many risks.

---

[22] For further information on supply strategies for low-demand parts in the Air Force, see Chenoweth, Arkes, and Moore (2010).

39

Many enterprises have recently begun to quantify the effects of various types of disruptions on the enterprise, products, and customers. Because supply chain managers must justify resources for SCRM, quantifying the prospective consequences of supply chain risks is important to its success.

Some enterprises are also requiring that key suppliers develop business-continuity plans, which are regularly reviewed (e.g., annually or every six months), and commit to a recovery time. Leading companies are developing standard, enterprise-wide metrics for SCRM and assessing business units and personnel on their plans. They are also establishing sense-and-respond mechanisms, often with the help of third parties that specialize in different types of SCRM events, such as supplier financial distress or natural disasters. Ideally, such efforts will prevent some disruptions before they happen or, should they occur anyway, help enterprises quickly identify supply chain disruptions, assess their consequence, and initiate recovery plans. Many firms are also turning to such organizations as the Supply Chain Risk Leadership Council (SCRLC) and its guidelines for help in managing supply chain risks (SCRLC, 2011).

Although leading purchasing-and-supply management practices can pose new risks, some may facilitate SCRM. Rationalizing the supply base and strategic sourcing often leads to fewer suppliers, which can make supply chains more brittle and increase the chance of supply disruption, making SCRM initiatives even more important. At the same time, having fewer suppliers can facilitate closer relationships with remaining key suppliers, and moving to higher-performing suppliers can facilitate a focus on continuous improvement. Having fewer contracts per supplier facilitates consistent terms and conditions, metrics, and relationships. Shifting to longer-term supplier relationships or contracts can facilitate broader partnerships, including commitment to develop business-continuity plans and time-to-recovery goals. Contracts with performance incentives facilitate both unilateral and joint continuous improvement initiatives.

Many leading supplier relationship management practices also facilitate SCRM. Strategically managing all business with each supplier rather than managing individual purchases can help the supplier to develop enterprise-wide business-continuity plans and time-to-recover commitments. Improved, closer communications with suppliers helps identify and proactively manage prospective supply chain risks. Using consistent performance objectives and metrics with a supplier can help embed SCRM in the relationship. Providing incentives for continuous supplier improvement facilitates proactive reduction in supply chain risks. Providing systematic supplier development facilitates specific goals and plans for SCRM improvement. Integrating key suppliers into key buyer processes expands SCRM options. Moving SCRM to upstream suppliers reduces end-to-end supply chain risks. The March 2011 Japan earthquake uncovered a key weakness in SCRM practices for many firms, which realized that they did not know their supplier's suppliers, many of whom were severely affected by the earthquake or resulting tsunami and nuclear contamination (Kim, 2012). Indeed, buyers have the ability to influence suppliers and to propagate SCRM best practices into upstream supply networks. Recent events, such as the horrific Japanese earthquake, tsunami, and nuclear disaster, have shown the importance of their doing so.

In the next chapter, we review DoD and Air Force guidance for supply chain risk management. We will pay particular attention to gaps between the best practices we identified above and DoD and Air Force practices in identifying and developing methods to manage supply chain risks and in enterprise-wide mechanisms to assess, analyze, and mitigate such risks.

4. Department of Defense and Air Force Guidance for Supply Chain Risk Management

DoD and the Air Force have several sources of guidance regarding supply chain risk management. Although not all are in one place, they address many of the supply chain risks the Air Force may face. We review these in this chapter and provide an integrated guide to them. We find that DoD addresses some supply chain risks and its suppliers address others, but a few supply chain risks are addressed by neither. Among these are environmental risks such as those caused by natural disasters or geopolitical events that are implicitly covered in *force majeure* clauses (excusing delay caused by events beyond the reasonable control of the contractor) of acquisition contracts. This means, in effect, that DoD has the responsibility for and must manage them.

In comparing the risks that DoD and Air Force guidance and interviews indicate are covered with an overall list of likely risks, we find a substantial set not directly addressed by DoD or the Air Force, even though the Federal Acquisition Regulation (FAR) explicitly absolves the supplier for responsibility of managing many of these (as in *force majeure* contract clauses).

Sources of Guidance on Risks for DoD

We identified DoD and Air Force guidance on supply chain risks through a literature review and interviews with DoD and Air Force personnel on "risk" during a weapon system's life cycle. The documents we reviewed included DoD Directive (DoDD) 5000.01, *The Defense Acquisition System*; DoD Instruction (DoDI) 5000.02, *Operation of the Defense Acquisition System*; the DoD *Risk Management Guide for DoD Acquisition* (Department of Defense, 2006); Air Force Instruction (AFI) 63-101, *Acquisition and Sustainment Life Cycle Management*; AFI 63-501, *Air Force Acquisition Quality Program*; DoDI 4140.1-R, the *DoD Supply Chain Materiel Management Regulation*; *USAF Deficiency Reporting, Investigation and Resolution* (Secretary of the Air Force, 2011); the Air Force's "Guidance Memorandum: Life Cycle Risk Management" (Payton, 2008); and the FAR.

We found that risk identification and mitigation strategies focus on activities during the acquisition phase and are related to risks in cost, technical performance, or schedule of the weapon system acquisition program. We found no direct discussion of risk in sustainment in Air Force guidance or how decisions about supply chain risk and supplier

43

relationship management made during the design phase could affect subsequent sustainment risks. We briefly describe each of these documents in Appendix E.

The FAR, governing the federal acquisition of goods and services, shapes supply chain risk management within DoD and among major OEMs.[23] The FAR governs the acquisition of products and services by agents of the federal government. It provides a consistent set of guidelines and legal definitions for establishing the obligations and responsibilities of contractors. Yet its discussion of risk focuses on cost, technical performance, and schedule, with no general reference to supply chain risk or specific reference to risks noted in literature on commercial practices.

The FAR provides that all federal contracts have a *force majeure* clause. This clause excuses delays

> . . . caused by an occurrence beyond the reasonable control of the Contractor and without its fault or negligence such as acts of God or the public enemy, acts of the Government in either its sovereign or contractual authority, fires, floods, epidemics, quarantine restrictions, strikes, unusually severe weather, and delays of common carriers.

The effect of this clause is to transfer many risks, including those for natural disasters, to the Air Force in its contracting. We saw in Figure 2.2 that aeronautics and defense firms were less likely than high-technology, chemical, and pharmaceutical firms, among others, to consider natural disasters as supply chain risks (Hillman and Keltz, 2007). This contractual transfer of many risks should be of substantial concern to weapon system program managers and supply chain managers within DoD and the Air Force. Without an SCRM plan that focuses on all key risks, the Air Force may be unprepared for such events and suffer greater duration and adverse consequences on readiness and operations should they occur.

We surmise that the *force majeure* clause of federal contracts, which aeronautics and defense firms are more likely than others to hold, may be one reason for this. As one aerospace SCRM official we interviewed told us, "One thing we look at is what is in the contract. If there is a *force majeure* clause, then the cost of realizing a supply chain disruption due to natural causes is passed on to the customer." Such clauses mean that suppliers are not held responsible for disruptions considered outside their control, but the customer bears the consequences and must wait for the supplier to resume operations.

The only DoD or Air Force guidance specific to supply chain risk is DoD 4140.1-R, *DoD Supply Chain Materiel Management Regulation*. The scope of risks identified in that guidance is limited to such sustainment issues as stock outages, stockpile

---

[23] The Defense Federal Acquisition Regulation Supplement guides DoD implementation of the FAR. It contains requirements of law, DoD-wide policies, delegations of FAR authorities, deviations from FAR requirements, and policies and procedures that have a significant effect on the public.

drawdowns, shelf-life expiration, supplier financial problems, long repair-cycle times, long order and shipping times, underestimating the true maintenance replacement rate, resupply from external sources such as direct vendor deliveries, and underutilization of existing inventory. Moreover, although DoD 4140.1-R identifies some categories of risks (e.g., retail stock level) and lists other potential contributors to risk, it does not discuss how to manage risks in any detail.

Overall, as Figure 4.1 shows, DoD and its suppliers actively manage only a portion of risks identified in the literature. (We remind the reader that Appendix B provides a more complete list of supply chain risks.) Its efforts to identify and manage risks such as "out of stock," "draw down of stockpile," and "shelf life expiration," match those, as highlighted in yellow, of "demand uncertainty" in the business literature. Its efforts to identify and manage risks such as those posed by external resupply, excessive times for order or repair, and high maintenance, replacement rates match those, as highlighted in orange, of leading businesses to identify and manage risks posed by long lead times and distribution and logistics delays or failures. DoD efforts to identify and manage supplier financial problems match those of leading businesses, as highlighted in green, to identify

**Figure 4.1. DoD and Its Suppliers Identify Some, But Not All, Risks
Identified in Business Literature**

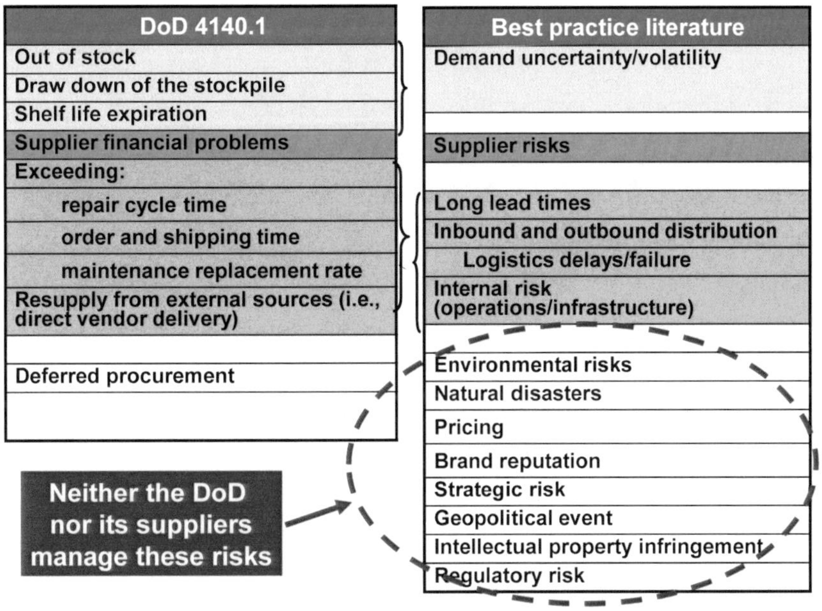

SOURCES: Office of the Deputy Under Secretary of Defense for Logistics and Materiel Readiness (2003); Enslow (2008); and Hillman and Keltz (2007).

45

and manage supplier risks. DoD efforts to address risks of underutilization of existing inventory have no strictly comparable match in the literature on best practices.

At the same time, several categories of risks identified in the business literature are not addressed by. These include "environmental," "natural disaster," "pricing," "brand reputation," "strategic," "geopolitical," "intellectual property infringement," and "regulatory risks." Some of these risks, such as "brand reputation," do not appear directly pertinent to the Air Force. Nevertheless, the overall comparison reveals a substantial set of risks not directly addressed by DoD or the Air Force, even though the FAR explicitly absolves the supplier of responsibility of managing many of them. Two questions arise from this analysis. First, what is the potential effect on the Air Force's supply chain from failing to manage these risks? Second, how does the Air Force currently implement guidance to manage identified risks?

Potential Effect on the Supply Chain from Failing to Manage Some Risks

To understand the potential consequences on the Air Force's supply chain from failing to manage risks, we consider risks from environmental causes (typically natural disasters). Figure 4.2, showing locations of weapon system contractors for product centers,[24] highlights areas susceptible to hurricane, tornado, or earthquake damage. We use fiscal year (FY) 2007 data from the Federal Procurement Data System (FPDS) for an exemplary analysis to identify the place of performance of suppliers of Air Force weapon systems. We circle clusters of suppliers with facilities in natural disaster risk zones. The fact that a supplier is located in a risk zone does not necessarily mean that the Air Force's weapon system supply chain is at risk. Nevertheless, such a location indicates the extent to which natural disasters could affect the Air Force supply chain, which policymakers and acquisition managers should understand when developing appropriate mitigation plans.

This map should lead policymakers and program managers to consider the following questions.

---

[24] At the time of this research the Air Force had three product centers, the Air Armament Center (AAC), the Aeronautical Systems Center (ASC), and the Electronic Systems Center (ESC). Under a subsequent reorganization, these three centers became the Air Force Life Cycle Management Center (AFLCMC) within the AFMC.

**Figure 4.2. Many Product Center Suppliers Are Located
in High-Risk Areas**

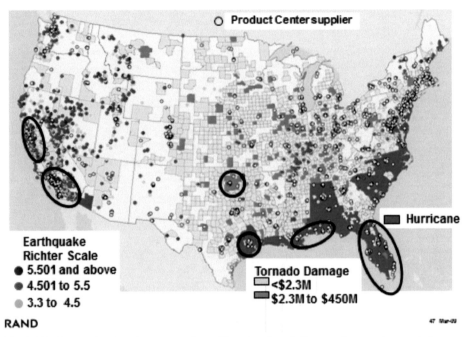

SOURCE: Created using the mapmaker utility at nationalatlas.gov/mapmaker and places
of performance from the FPDS.
NOTE: Such analysis is exemplary and can be updated with more recent information on
threats and suppliers.

- Which goods and services are produced by the suppliers at risk for natural disasters?
- Which weapon system do these goods and services affect?
- If a supplier experiences *force majeure*, what will be its time to recovery?
- Who in the Air Force has this information?
- Do the suppliers have business-continuity plans in place, and has the Air Force reviewed the plans to determine their adequacy?

Air Force Guidelines and Implementation in Practice

To understand how the Air Force currently practices supply chain risk management in light of its guidance, we include Figure 4.3, based on the 2008 version of DoDI 5000.02 (2008), which illustrates concurrent guidance for life cycle management from four

Figure 4.3. Integration of Sustainment and Acquisition Functions in Air Force Life Cycle Guidance

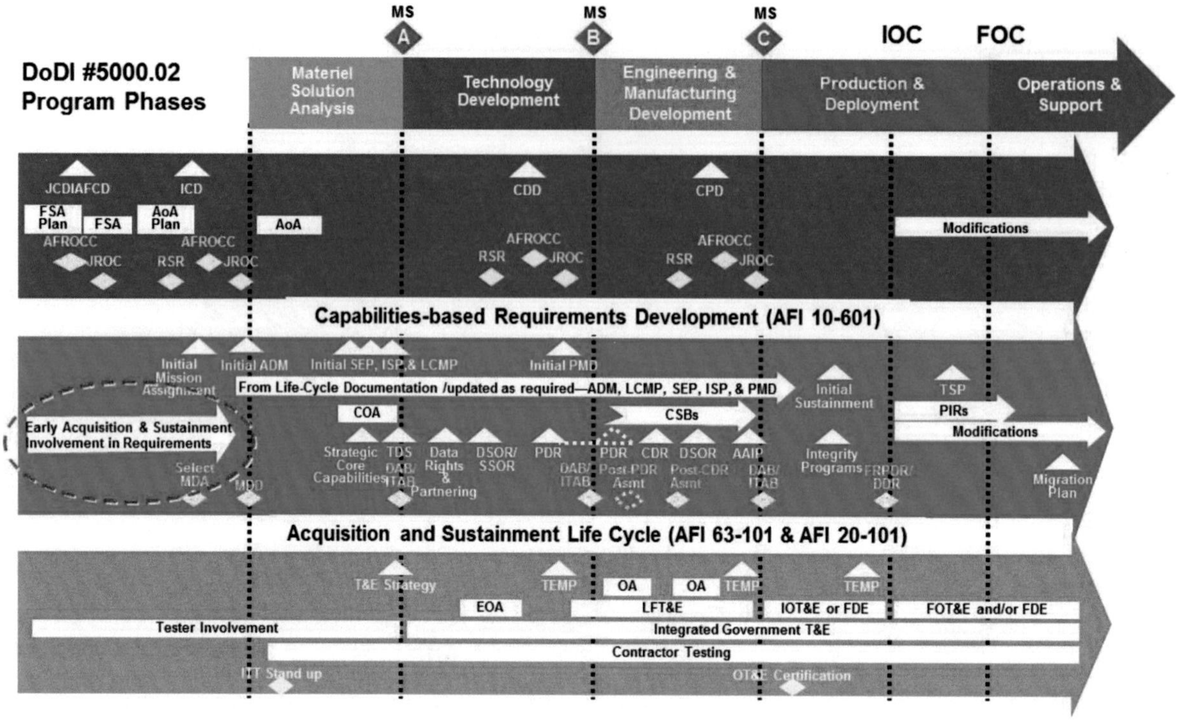

SOURCE: DoDI 5000.02 (2008).

different DoD and Air Force documents: DoDI 5000.02 (2008), AFI 10-601 (2006), AFI 63-101 (2009), and AFI 20-101 (2012).[25]

In 2009, Air Force policymakers acknowledged the need to begin planning for weapon system sustainment early in acquisition. AFI 63-101 (2009) describes the Integrated Life Management Cycle, noting, "The sustainment community, in collaboration with the user, needs to address reliability, availability and maintainability to ensure life-cycle mission capability and supportability." To minimize risks throughout the weapon system life cycle, including sustainment, this step should be concurrent with the Initial Capabilities Document (ICD) and the analysis of alternatives (AoA) and occur before the program entering the materiel solution phase.[26]

---

[25] Note that we used several versions of these documents at the time of our research, and that some have since been updated. Specifically, we used the July 31, 2006, version of AFI 10-601, which was updated on July 12, 2010, and the April 7, 2009, version of AFI 63-101, which was revised in August 2011.

[26] Other activities occurring before materiel solution analysis are the integration of the Joint Capabilities Document/Air Force Capabilities Document, the functional solutions analysis, review by the Air Force Requirements for Operational Capabilities Council (AFROCC) and the Joint Requirements Oversight Council (JROC), the requirements strategy review (RSR), the initial mission assignment, and selection of

Almost all phases of the weapon system life cycle plan involve collaboration between the program management office, the OEM, and subtier suppliers. Ideally, the end user (i.e., requirements generator) will help make trade-offs. Suppliers must demonstrate capabilities at several key steps.

DoD 5000.02 (2008) states that during technology development, before Milestone (MS) B, programs should take steps to "reduce technology risk, determine the appropriate technology set of technologies . . . demonstrate critical technology elements on prototypes, and complete a preliminary design." Concurrent with this program phase, AFI 63-101 (2009) states that depot source of repair (DSOR) and strategic source of repair (SSOR) activities take place requiring a decision on "all depot-level maintenance for hardware and software, with special attention to Title 10 USC 2464 (Core Capability) and Title 10 USC §2466 (50/50 Requirements)." Not stated directly, but implied, is that contractors may provide some sustainment directly through PBL arrangements or other contracting instruments.[27]

Before Milestone C, during engineering and manufacturing development, DoD 5000.02 (2008) requires steps to "validate producibility and manufacturing processes; posture for life cycle sustainment; ensure affordability; and demonstrate system integration, interoperability, safety and utility." The Capability Production Document establishes measurable and testable requirements necessary to support production and sustainment. DoD 5000.02 (2008) further states that, before entering production and deployment, the critical design review (CDR) validate that all system of system functionality and interfaces have been worked through and that all hardware and software requirements are defined.[28]

---

the Milestone Decision Authority(MDA). Additional steps as the materiel solution analysis launches or proceeds are the initial Acquisition Decision Memorandum, Systems Engineering Plan, Information Support Plan, and Life Cycle Management Plan; development of courses of action, strategic core capabilities, and the Technology Development Strategy; review by the Defense Acquisition Board (DAB) and the Information Technology Advisory Board (ITAB); and launching of the tester involvement, the integrated test team, contractor testing, and the test and evaluation (T&E) strategy.

[27] Other activities during technology development before Milestone B affecting life-cycle planning include issue of the Capability Development Document; an RSR and additional reviews by the JROC, AFROCC, DAB, and ITAB for information technology systems; the initial Program Management Directive; establishment of data rights and partnering; the preliminary design review (PDR); development of the Test and Evaluation Master Plan (TEMP); early operational assessment; initiation of integrated government T&E and of live fire test and evaluation (LFT&E); and continued contractor testing.

[28] Other activities during engineering and manufacturing development include additional requirements strategy reviews and additional reviews by the JROC, AFROCC, DAB, and ITAB; formation of Configuration Steering Boards; conclusion of the PDR; DSOR involvement; development of an Aircraft Availability and Improvement Program; post-CDR assessment; an additional DSOR; operational assessments; TEMP development and review; and continued LFT&E, integrated government T&E, and contractor testing.

As the system enters production and deployment and approaches initial operational capability and full operational capability, the program manager leads the integration of production and support activities. At this point, according to AFI 63-101 (2009), there is "significant support" from the user and sustainment communities to ensure an orderly transition from production to operation.[29]

Although suppliers are involved in many critical phases of weapon system acquisition, there is no direct call in Air Force guidance to assess supplier risk, whether from exposure to natural disasters, financial instability, or some other source. Nevertheless, Air Force and DoD guidance requires integration of sustainment issues early in the acquisition process. The existing framework could be expanded to specifically address a variety of supply chain risks. The Air Force and DoD have also acquired greater visibility into suppliers' suppliers. As a result of the 2006 Federal Funding Accountability and Transparency Act (FFATA), the government now has visibility into prime contractor first-tier subawards greater than $25,000 through the FFATA Subaward Reporting System.

Our findings concur with those of a Comprehensive National Cybersecurity Initiative SCRM Implementation Plan (Davidson, 2009) and a SCRM Directive Type Memo (DTM) DTM-09-016 of March 25, 2010 (Lynn, 2010).

The Comprehensive National Cybersecurity Initiative (CNCI) Global SCRM Strategy and Implementation Plan found significant gaps in U.S. government policy regarding SCRM. The CNCI study details the growing supply chain risk posed by non-U.S. control of cyber design and manufacturing. The issues it identified were

- no mandate to address supply chain risk
- limited tools to manage risk
- lack of guidance and governance for SCRM.

SCRM DTM guidance (Lynn, 2010) establishes policy and calls for DoD acquisitions, technology, and logistics personnel to coordinate with DoD components in developing pilot programs to manage supply chain risk. Of special concern is supply chain risk related to information technology and how it creates vulnerabilities in the Global Information Grid essential to accomplishing DoD's mission. The document also establishes processes and controls to

---

[29] Activities supporting these and subsequent phases include Initial Sustainment and Integrity Programs; the team software process; post implementation reviews; the full rate production decision review and the detail design review; the migration plan; the initial operational test and evaluation, full deployment evaluation, or follow-on test and evaluation; continued integrated government T&E; continued contractor testing; and operational test and evaluation certification.

- ensure that intelligence assessments are conducted in accordance with applicable laws and regulations
- assess threats from potential suppliers providing critical information and communication technology components to covered systems
- manage the quality, configuration, and security of software, hardware, and systems throughout their life cycles, including components or subcomponents from secondary sources
- detect the occurrence, reduce the likelihood, and mitigate the consequences of products containing counterfeit components or malicious functions
- ensure that integrated circuits custom-designed or manufactured for a specific DoD end use are made by accredited suppliers of integrated circuit-related services.

In the next chapter, we summarize our findings from a number of weapon system case studies regarding Air Force SCRM in the acquisition and sustainment phases of a weapon system's life cycle.

5. Air Force SCRM Case Studies

How has the Air Force actually practiced supply chain risk management? In this chapter, we explore the documented processes for managing supply chain risk. We seek to identify which supply chain risks are considered throughout the weapon system life cycle, how they are managed, and who in the Air Force is responsible for managing them. To explore these issues, we reviewed Air Force data on procurement and interviewed Air Force personnel in weapon system management, commodity councils, F-16 maintenance organizations, and C-17 managers, among others.

Our analyses of contract-action data show that contractors typically have multiple contracts and that the proportion of dollars spent on long-term contracts has decreased whereas that on short-term contracts has increased. Many short-term contracts may inhibit development of supplier relationships facilitating better supply chain risk management. Our interviews revealed that Air Force supply chain risk management is often reactive. We also found that acquisition and sustainment personnel tended to consider different risks—and that they also typically did not address some distribution risks.

Air Force Contract Action Data

We analyzed product center and Air Logistics Center (ALC) contract actions from FY 1995 to FY 2010 to identify any trends in contracting practices that support SCRM.[30] The ALCs reduced their number of suppliers by about a third during this time, but the product centers slightly increased their supplier base (Table 5.1). There was also little change in the percentage of product center contracts or dollars that were sole-source, but those for ALCs decreased. The ALCs saw their number of contracts per supplier decrease by more than one-fourth, but there was no change in the number of contracts per supplier for the product centers. The proportion of expenditures through long-term contracts decreased for the product centers and the ALCs , whereas those for short-term contracts increased. Finally, only a small proportion of product center and ALC contracts have performance incentives. This suggests that product center and ALC contracting practices could be improved, particularly in reducing the number of suppliers and sole-source contracts, the number of contracts per supplier, and the proportion of dollars spent in short-term contracts. In particular, reducing the number of contracts per supplier and increasing the

---

[30] We reference product centers and ALCs here, since these data predate AFMC's reorganization.

Table 5.1. Data Suggest That Product Center and ALC Contracting Practices May Not Support Best SCRM

	Product Center Contracts > $25,000		Air Logistics Center Contracts > $25,000	
	FY 1995	FY 2010	FY 1995	FY 2010
Number of suppliers	1,452	1,484	2,375	1,558
Sole-source contracts (and dollars)	32% (62%)	33% (59%)	46% (58%)	32% (48%)
Contracts per supplier	2.0	2.0	3.0	2.2
Dollars on long-term (> 5 years) contracts	18%	13%	23%	19%
Dollars on short-term contracts (< 2 years)	9%	54%	34%	58%
Contracts (and dollars) with performance incentives	5% (38%)	2% (11%)	1% (10%)	1% (10%)

proportion of dollars on long-term, performance-based contracts could facilitate more collaborative supplier relationships that improve SCRM irrespective of reducing the number of suppliers.

Interview Findings: Acquisition

To gather information about supply chain risk management during acquisition, we interviewed personnel from six weapon system program offices, selected from sponsor recommendations and representing a wide range of SCRM issues. Four of the systems were Air Force weapon systems and two were joint systems. Most had single prime contractors, but two had multiple contractors, and their suppliers were both U.S. and foreign. Our interviewees had experience in logistics, acquisition, program management, engineering, maintenance, and operations.

Our interviews of acquisition personnel lasted one to two hours. We interviewed 15 persons total, between one and six per interview, to all of whom we promised anonymity. We used structured but open-ended questions that encouraged respondents to share their individual experience while keeping a focus on supply chain risk management. The open-ended format also permitted us to ask additional questions as they arose. We had three researchers at each interview, all taking notes, to ensure a comprehensive recounting when we later compiled our notes from the interviews.

Our interviewees made clear that weapon programs use a range of approaches to risk management. Two mentioned using a risk matrix, as shown in Figure 3.4, as a central element of the *Defense Acquisition Guidebook* (Department of Defense, 2008).

Some interviewees emphasized the role of performance-based contracts, including incentives or penalties, in risk management. For these interviewees, risk management was largely the responsibility of the contractor. These interviewees viewed risks such as natural disasters, from which contractors are exempt, as virtually impossible to mitigate and low in likelihood. Interviewees pointed to resource constraints as one reason not to manage such risks, saying

> Some of them [risks], to be honest, are always in the back of your mind, but what can we do about them? I was looking at those external risks there. For the most part, when we sit down and do our risk analysis, none of those are really going to be on our list.

An interviewee from one joint program described a more involved and comprehensive risk management effort than most others did. The program's approach of "modified Willoughby templates" included mitigation strategies for "risk areas associated with design, test, production, facilities, logistics, management, and funding."[31] Although not part of Air Force guidance, these are part of Navy policy (Department of the Navy, 1986).

Despite these specific approaches, the most common theme across the interviews was a reactive approach to managing risk. That is, interviewees reported learning how to deal with a problem after it has arisen and trying to prevent it before it arises again, rather than proactively identifying and mitigating risks before they occur. Respondents often defaulted to this approach for any risks that they did not actively manage. They identified resource constraints and low probability as the biggest reasons for a reactive approach. Even though the *Risk Management Guide for DoD Acquisition* (Department of Defense, 2006) explicitly distinguishes between "risk management" (future) and "issue management" (current and past), reacting to problems that have occurred was considered managing risk to many we interviewed. One respondent even claimed

> The biggest impediment to risk management—my personal opinion—is that DoD doesn't understand what risk is. When things have already happened, they are no longer risk, they are reality. We spend a lot of time talking about reality. . . . It doesn't prepare you for the future. . . . Risk is things that may happen, and risk management is your plans to try to avoid or mitigate it. They talk a good talk, but what they [. . .[32]] is not risk, it's reality.

---

[31] Willoughby templates help verify that projects have "not overlooked any potential risk areas associated with design, test, production, facilities, logistics, management, and funding." For further information, see Defense Acquisition University, 2012.

[32] Word not clear.

One reason that approaches to managing risk vary so widely is likely because programs do not appear to be using the same policy guidance. Interviewees from three of six programs identified the DoD 5000 series by name, but only one mentioned specifics about its use. Interviewees from one of the joint programs referenced Navy policy guidance, whereas those in another program identified guidance that the local base had developed. Interviewees from the remaining two programs were unable to identify their reference policy for risk management. Altogether, our findings suggest that the available guidance for managing risk is either not well understood or is not useful. Either way, it is not widely used.

We also asked program managers and their staff about two sets of activities in the acquisition process. First, we asked about risk management during each of the 49 major activities and processes outlined in the DoD Acquisition Guidebook (5000.1). These included concept-refinement documents and activities leading to Milestone A, technology-development documents and activities leading to Milestone B, supportability and logistics-consideration documents and activities involved in system development and demonstration and in production and deployment, and other processes. (The specific activities and processes are listed in Question 6 of the interview protocol in Appendix D.) In a separate set of questions, we asked about the eight issues related to support that make up the total system product support package, also in the DoD Acquisition Guidebook. These are supply support (spare/repair parts), maintenance planning, test/support equipment, technical documentation/interactive electronic technical manuals, manpower and training/computer based training, facilities, packaging handling storage and transportation, and design interface/computing support.

We found that personnel familiar with these different activities had varying levels of experience with them. Regardless of level of experience with a given activity, however, we found no common approach to supply chain risk among our interviewees. Interviewees differed by the activities in which they considered supply chain risk and some did not consider managing risk much in any of the activities.

We also received mixed responses on how much the various programs required of suppliers regarding risk management and how closely they worked with suppliers to manage risk. Two of the programs required that their OEMs have business-continuity plans, although these did not necessarily identify individual risks or specify the time it would take to recover. Three programs reported not requiring risk management plans, and two did not answer the question.

We asked about risk management required from subcontractors as well, and learned that few programs required it. One reason for this is that standard subcontracting plans do not address supply chain risk; their primary aim is to assure small business participation.

Nonetheless, two programs reported requiring that their OEM address supply chain risk in subcontracting.

We also asked how much the programs worked with their suppliers regarding supply chain risk. Many programs used both their own personnel and DCMA for on-site surveillance of their suppliers. Interviewees of one program that had a foreign company as prime contractor also used the equivalent of DCMA in the country where the prime contractor was located. Some of this on-site work was problem-specific, reacting to situations as they arose. As one respondent put it, "Most of the agreements I've been on have had DCMA be our eyes and ears at the plant. . . . I think if an issue came up, we would have [our] people there and work on it. I can't recall anything pro-active." Other programs had regular, ongoing interactions with their suppliers, with one respondent explaining, "I would say that our program does better than most because I have a detachment co-located with [supplier]. They can be on the floor and get insight into what's going on."

Visibility on upstream suppliers[33] also varied but was mostly reactive. One person spoke the sentiment of many when he said, "Unless you're willing to put a hundred people in the program office, you're never going to have [much upstream] visibility." At the same time, some programs worked to have as much visibility and influence on the subcontractors as they could get to mitigate risks and solve problems. One person who worked in both acquisition and sustainment said, "We don't direct the subs—it's the prime's responsibility—but we go in and say, 'We've got guys in combat, and we need eight repairs this month, not four. How can we get that?'"

Interview Findings: Sustainment

We conducted research on sustainment SCRM in industry (Moore and Loredo, 2013). We also sought to understand the processes used by the Air Force to manage supply chain risks during sustainment. We wanted to identify which supply chain sustainment risks are known, how they are managed, and who in the Air Force is responsible for managing them. To answer these questions, we spoke with representatives of the F-16 sustainment organization and of Boeing's C-17 PBL management office. We also visited the C-17 sustainment wing at Warner Robins Air Force Base, Georgia, and spoke to representatives there about C-17 sustainment activities and their relationship with Boeing. We interviewed DLA personnel by phone regarding the role of the DLA in Air Force sustainment SCRM. We also interviewed subject-matter experts in the Air Force

---

[33] Upstream visibility as used here refers to the identity of prime contractors' subcontractors, subcontractors to the prime contractors' subcontractors, and the specific inputs of all subcontractors to the final product.

Commodity Councils at each of the Air Logistics Centers, Ogden, Oklahoma City, and Warner Robins. Questions we sought to answer about F-16 and C-17 SCRM included the following:

- Is there a clearly discernible SCRM process?
- Which supply chain risks are considered, and how are they prioritized?
- What may impede development of a SCRM process?

We found that each ALC had a slightly different approach to SCRM. These differences are a result of the type of commodities they manage, the amount of previous exposure to supply chain problems, and perceived reasons for those problems that each ALC has.

For example, the Landing Gear Commodity Council (LGCC) deals with many more competitively sourced parts than does the Aircraft Structures or Propulsion Commodity Council. Therefore, most of its SCRM focuses on mitigating risks in managing the deliverables of multiple suppliers. In some cases, landing-gear components were experiencing production lead times of 900 to 1,000 days, or nearly three years. Many landing-gear items are provided by small businesses; indeed, DoD met many small business goals through purchase of these items. The effort required to manage all these small businesses is significant, especially in light of Air Force personnel reductions.

To mitigate the risk created by long lead times and the difficulty of managing many small business suppliers, the LGCC has developed a prime vendor approach, in which the prime vendor manages the deliverables of other suppliers. This strategy transfers responsibility and risk from the Air Force and to a lead supplier or prime vendor. Although many contractors are involved, a lead contractor is responsible for the final on-time or specified delivery of the item. This lets the Air Force consolidate contracts under one supplier, thereby permitting greater visibility of performance problems. Perhaps more important, the lead supplier integrator has strong incentives to act quickly to correct performance problems. Air Force representatives noted that the supplier integrator has more leeway in terminating contracts for lack of performance by individual suppliers than the Air Force would have. In this case, the Air Force has knowingly transferred responsibility for a critical supply chain performance criterion (delivery lead times) to an external supplier. The commodity councils have weighed the risk of transferring this responsibility against the benefits of the streamlined management structure it affords and have decided to assume the risk. The Air Force is aware of the transfer risk and has chosen to mitigate it, namely through incentives and penalties on the lead supplier based on performance of the subtier suppliers.

Representatives of the Aircraft Structures Commodity Council and the Communications and Electronics Commodity Council told us that they examined the financial status of suppliers, especially those that had previously done business with DoD. This included using records of the Defense Contract Audit Agency to verify contractor performance on previous government contracts but seldom included other financial rating systems, such as Dun and Bradstreet and Capital One. High-value or competitive contracts typically had more thorough financial examinations, but for more than 95 percent of acquisitions financial checks ended with the Defense Contract Audit Agency clearance.

Commodity council representatives also recognized several other risks and related issues, including

- cost trade-offs between sole and multiple sources
- production quality
- not owning technical drawings
- ability to shift from first article test to production
- ability to manufacture including tooling and personnel skills.

Although the commodity councils recognize these risks and related issues, they do not mitigate them directly. Rather, they remain focused on managing contracts. The commodity councils are aware of many risks but have no systematic method for identifying, assessing, and mitigating risks other than contractual risk.

Table 5.2 summarizes the findings from our interviews among F-6, C-17, commodity councils, and DLA personnel regarding sustainment SCRM. We discuss each of these below.

F-16 SCRM

F-16 sustainment relies on organic depots for repairs and maintenance, on the ALCs for management of inventory and purchases of repaired parts from depots and outside contractors, and on DLA for the purchase of new depot-level repairables and consumable parts for repairs and replacements. These primary suppliers each have their own supply chain. Under this arrangement, F-16 supply chain risks can be effectively managed if one assumes that each stakeholder will adequately manage its own supply chain risks, that important risks are known to key stakeholders, and that risk mitigation focuses on improving the reliability of the F-16's supply chain. If any of these assumptions are false then SCRM for the F-16 is ineffective.

Multiple organizations involved in managing supply chain risks may not have the same incentives or priorities. For example, we will discuss below how DLA seeks to reduce its inventory footprint and its willingness to increase the risk of not having a low-demand part available, whereas the Air Force is willing to pay the cost for holding slow-moving inventory if it reduces the risk of stock outages.

Table 5.2. Sustainment SCRM Processes and Objectives

	F-16 Sustainment	C-17/Boeing Lead System Integrator	Commodity Council	DLA (for DLA-Managed Parts in Air Force Sustainment)
SCRM process	• No separate, distinct SCRM	• Boeing guidance • Integrated processes • ISO certification and business-continuity plans	• No separate, distinct SCRM	• Does not consider supply chain risk
Objectives	• Integrated process teams manage supplier relations and react to problems • Quality • Financial (contract) • Reduce delivery times	• Financial • Quality • Capacity • Past performance	• Facilitate and manage contracts for commodities • 8-step process for establishing contracts provides guidelines for managing contract risk	• Reduces inventory footprint • Invest in "slow-moving" or "low-demand" items
Other issues	• Guidance and training do not support SCRM • Limited visibility of supply chain	• *Force majeure* clause exempts responsibility when supply chain failure is a result of "acts of God," fires, strikes, wars, etc.	• "Risk" mitigation focuses on establishing contracts for commodities	• Reduces inventory to reduce cost • Unilateral decisionmaking on non-system-coded parts • Some coordination with Air Force

SCRM Process

The F-16 sustainment branch participates in quarterly integrated process team (IPT) meetings to discuss concerns and issues. Nevertheless, no IPTs specifically discuss supply chain risks. The F-16 team works with suppliers to develop and maintain supplier relations, but limitations on manpower availability and data at the sustainment-wing level limit proactive SCRM efforts.

Objectives

F-16 SCRM is mostly reactive; if an event such as a wildfire is threatening a supplier, Air Force managers will call the supplier to assess the level of threat. We could discern no strategic-level supply chain risk assessment or mitigation beyond such ad hoc efforts. The concerns at the wing level are with the quality of the repair or manufacture, existence of a contract or financial arrangement to obtain the needed part, and delivery lead times. We saw very little evidence of a purposely designed and implemented SCRM process.

Other Issues

Implementing such a process at this level of the Air Force organizational structure is challenging. The sustainment wing does not have the personnel, training, or access to data needed to implement an SCRM process. It would also likely lack the leverage needed to work with suppliers and to change suppliers' existing supply chain management processes. There are two reasons for this. First, wing-level maintenance often does not have enough volume of demand to influence suppliers. Second, many supply decisions are made in the acquisition phase, meaning that they cannot be changed in the sustainment phase.

C-17/Boeing SCRM

At the time of our research, the C-17 supply chain was managed by Boeing Corporation, which served as the lead system integrator (LSI) responsible for C-17 sustainment. A PBL contract between the Air Force and Boeing set performance expectations and compensation for Boeing as the LSI. Under this agreement, Boeing entered into contracts with the Air Force's organic depots, commercial suppliers, and DLA. The effectiveness of the LSI arrangement was judged by performance metrics. Boeing took full responsibility for supplier selection, inventory levels of all C-17 unique parts, and the distribution of parts. Boeing owns the demand history and the forecast method for the C-17 parts it manages. Boeing conducted SCRM based on its own judgment and prioritization of risk. It also managed and owned data on system performance. Boeing, and not the Air Force, had the direct relationships with subtier suppliers. Our C-17 sustainment-wing interviewees at Warner Robins reported difficulties establishing relationships with Boeing's subtier suppliers for the maintenance workloads that were under depot management.

SCRM Process

Because the PBL contract granted Boeing full responsibility over C-17 sustainment decisions, it also granted Boeing responsibility over SCRM. We interviewed members of Boeing's C-17 sustainment support team and asked how they conducted supply chain risk management. We did not find a discrete process for assessing and mitigating the C-17's supply chain risk. Rather, members of Boeing's C-17 sustainment team indicated that they followed corporate guidelines for managing risk.

We also spoke with a Boeing corporate representative about supply chain management strategy. This representative reported that at the corporate level, Boeing has a council on supply chain management across its major business units, which reports to the chief executive officer on supply chain matters. The council meets monthly and issues guidance on supplier selection and management. Supply chain risk is managed at the applicable program or business-division level and is implicitly part of the supplier performance reports.

Objectives

Boeing obtains and periodically reviews supplier information for risk assessments, including financial performance, quality, capacity, and past performance on cost, timeliness, and quality. It tracks performance over time to discern early indicators of any problems. It segregates suppliers by strategic importance. Its targets for key performance metrics vary by supplier. It assesses risks as part of its supplier-selection and ongoing supplier-management processes.

Boeing's supplier-selection process focuses on product quality and the supplier's financial position. Boeing verifies that the supplier is ISO-certified and is technically capable of doing the work required; such certification indicates the supplier's ability to deliver a quality product. Boeing also examines the supplier's financial risk; if it is deemed to be high but the supplier is critical, then Boeing tracks the supplier's financial performance monthly or quarterly.

Once the supplier is selected, Boeing stresses the quality and timeliness of supplier performance. For example, Boeing looks at the number of parts returned to a supplier because of a quality deficiency or discrepancy. Boeing also looks at turnaround times for repairs and manufacturing lead times. Boeing aggregates supplier performance metrics for quality and timeliness across business units and reports them enterprise-wide. Boeing Integrated Defense Systems personnel also know how suppliers are performing on Boeing commercial airplane contracts.

Other Issues

Boeing expects suppliers to be ISO-certified and assumes that they have business-continuity plans to resume work after disruption by disasters or other risk events. Boeing does not ask to see or certify suppliers' business-continuity plans. Asked why Boeing does not do so, Boeing representatives responded that, although they are concerned with work interruptions, they will work with suppliers to minimize their consequences and duration. If the work interruption were caused by a natural disaster, then the *force majeure* clause that flows down to subcontractors from prime contracts would exempt the supplier and Boeing from financial responsibility. This is effectively an insurance policy against unpredictable events for which Boeing did not have to insure.

Interviewees from the C-17 sustainment office at Boeing could not point to a product or report covering C-17 supply chain risk management. We conclude from other interviews that Boeing does have an SCRM process, but that it is not described or implemented separately. Rather, it is integrated into other processes such as supplier selection and management. Information about the performance of key suppliers is reported to the upper levels of management. When necessary, Boeing has onsite representation at the supplier facility to oversee supplier performance.

Commodity Councils

We found no separate, distinct SCRM process for commodity councils. The objectives of commodity councils are to develop sustainment supply strategies that support aircraft maintenance and repair for categories of goods and services. These should reduce costs through the use of strategic sourcing by reducing administrative and production lead times and improving on-time delivery (Kempf, 2012). Commodity councils manage contract risk through an eight-step process used for establishing contracts. Consequently, their risk mitigation is focused on contract risk. (For further details, see Appendix F.)

DLA

We also did not find evidence of supply chain risk considerations at DLA. Our interviewees there focused on an ongoing initiative to reduce inventory footprint, particularly for "slow-moving" or "low-demand" items. Cost reduction was their primary emphasis. They were making unilateral inventory decisions on non-weapon system coded parts inventories, with little consideration of future risks to availability. They were coordinating somewhat with the Air Force, particularly for weapon system coded parts.

Assessing Attention to Specific Risks

After our interviews, we asked acquisition and sustainment personnel to fill out a matrix of supply chain risks. We gave them a list of 36 general supply chain risks and 157 detailed risks and asked them to report which they consider during their work. Acquisition personnel reported considering more risks than sustainment personnel did. Yet even acquisition personnel reported that they do not typically consider supply chain risks in depth or even manage them, given their other risk priorities, i.e., cost, schedule, and technology. Below, we summarize responses (three from sustainment commodity managers and six from acquisition weapon system programs) regarding the general supply chain risks. (For more detail on supply chain risks that sustainment and acquisition personnel consider, see Appendix B.)

The results below show the average response among the following possible answers:

1 – never considered
2 – rarely considered
3 – considered half the time

4 – often considered

5 – always considered (high risk).

Table 5.3 lists supplier risks that were always or often considered in the acquisition phase.[34] We classify risks here as physical and regulatory risks, production problems, financial/cost losses, and management risks. The middle column indicates how frequently weapon system program personnel indicated such risks, and the right column indicates how often personnel considered them in the sustainment phase. Weapon system program personnel consider all these risks always or often. Sustainment personnel consider most of them only rarely or never and none of them more than half the time. One reason for this, sustainment personnel noted, is that by the time weapon systems move to sustainment, many parts have only one supplier—and sustainment personnel do not believe that there is much they can do to manage sole-source supplier risks.

Table 5.3. Physical, Regulatory, Production, Financial, and Management Supplier Risks Considered Always or Often by Weapon System Program Personnel

Supplier Risks	Acquisition	Sustainment
Physical and Regulatory Risks		
Material Unavailability/Lack of Planning	4	3
Legal Noncompliance	4	1
Regulatory Noncompliance	5	2
Production Problems		
Lack of Capacity	5	3
Technological Inadequacies or Failures	5	1
Poor Quality	5	3
Financial/cost Losses		
Competitive Pressures	5	1
Financial Viability	5	2
Management Risks		
Management Quality	5	2
Lack of Continuous Improvement	4	2
Lead Times	5	2
Poor Communication	4	3
Upstream Supply Risks	5	1
4,5 Always or Often 3 Half the time 1,2 Rarely or Never		

---

[34] We organize the subsequent figures and discussion of them by phases of the weapon system. We chose risk categories based on the literature regarding risks that enterprises consider and manage.

64

Similarly, Table 5.4 indicates that weapon system program personnel often or always consider risks associated with the buying enterprise, in this case the Air Force. Personnel responsible for the sustainment phase are less likely to consider these as well. Nevertheless, sustainment personnel do consider four buying-enterprise risks—demand volatility, design uncertainty, testing unavailability or inferiority, and supplier-relationship management use—often or always.

Weapon system program personnel also considered several distribution risks, such as cargo damage/theft/tampering and long, multiparty supply pipelines, as Table 5.5 indicates. Weapon system program personnel also reported that they consider four external risks—related to labor, legal, technology, and market issues—always or often. Personnel responsible for sustainment reported considering these risks never, rarely, or no more than half the time.

Some categories of risks weapon system program personnel considered less often. Table 5.6 shows that weapon system program personnel consider external risks related to natural disasters, accidents, political uncertainty, sabotage, terrorism, crime, or war no more than half the time. Personnel responsible for sustainment reported that they rarely or never considered these risks; believing that they could do nothing to prevent or prepare for them, they largely reacted to them. Weapon system program personnel also reported

**Table 5.4. Buying-Enterprise Risks Considered Always or Often
by Weapon System Program Personnel**

Buying Enterprise Risks	Acquisition	Sustainment
Demand Volatility	4	4
Personnel Unavailability/Lack of skill	5	3
Design Uncertainty	5	4
Planning Failures	5	3
Financial Uncertainty/Losses	5	3
Facility Unavailability/Unreliability	4	2
Testing Unavailability/Inferiority	5	5
Enterprise Underperformance/Lack of Value	5	2
Supplier Relationship Management Use	4	4

4.5	Always or Often	3	Half the time	1.2	Rarely or Never

**Table 5.5. Distribution of External Risks Considered Always or Often
by Weapon System Program Personnel**

Distribution Risks	Acquisition	Sustainment
Cargo Damage/Theft/Tampering	5	2
Long, Multi-Party Supply Pipelines	4	2

External Risks	Acquisition	Sustainment
Labor Unavailability and Lack of Skill	5	2
Lawsuits	5	1
Technological Uncertainty	5	3
Market Challenges	4	3

4.5 Always or Often	3 Half the time	1.2 Rarely or Never

**Table 5.6. Distribution of External Risks Considered Half the Time
by Weapon System Program Personnel**

External Risks	Acquisition	Sustainment
Natural Disasters	3	1
Accidents	3	1
Sabotage, Terrorism, Crime, and War	3	1
Government Compliance and Political Uncertainty	3	2

Distribution Risks	Acquisition	Sustainment
Warehouse Unavailability/Insecurity	3	-

4.5 Always or Often	3 Half the time	1.2 Rarely or Never

that they consider the distribution risk of warehouse unavailability/insecurity about half the time. We did not collect any data from sustainment personnel on this risk.

Finally, as Table 5.7 shows, both acquisition and sustainment personnel rarely or never considered three areas of distribution risks: infrastructure unavailability, vehicle accidents/lack of capacity, and labor unrest/unavailability.

Altogether, we found that acquisition processes are more focused on supply chain risks than sustainment processes are. Nevertheless, although acquisition personnel

**Table 5.7. Distribution of Risks Rarely or Never Considered
by Weapon System Program Personnel**

Distribution Risks	Acquisition	Sustainment
Infrastructure Unavailability	2	1
Vehicle Accidents/Lack of Capacity	2	1
Labor Unrest/Unavailability	2	1

4.5 Always or Often	3 Half the time	1.2 Rarely or Never

consider more supply chain risks than sustainment personnel do, they also reported that they do not consider risks in depth, nor do they fully manage those they do consider. Consequently, most acquisition and sustainment SCRM is largely reactive, focusing on damage control of supply chain disruptions that have already occurred rather than proactive mitigation of potential disruptions. Personnel do not have the incentives, tools, or time to proactively manage supply chain risks.

Summary of Case Studies

Taken together, the case studies show that SCRM is not practiced consistently across the Air Force, and, where it is practiced, it is often not sufficient. Weapon system managers reported a lack of enterprise-wide SCRM procedures and mechanisms. They also differed in the extent to which they considered supply chain risks, and few had mitigation plans for such risks. As a result, SCRM is usually in the form of reacting to a problem and not in actually planning for and mitigating a risk.

One likely reason for this lack of proactive SCRM may be weapon system milestone reviews, which do not specifically consider supply chain risks. As discussed in Table 2.1, SCRM is largely viewed as a future (i.e., long-term) sustainment responsibility rather than something to avoid or reduce during product design and manufacturing. Indeed, we found no SCRM links between design, manufacturing, and sustainment in practice. Because personnel responsible for acquisition do not know what those in sustainment do about supply chain risks, supply chain risk seems almost nonexistent.

Our SCRM case studies reinforced the finding from our review of guidance and policy that incentives to manage short-term acquisition risks override those for managing long-term supply chain risks. Our research also led to two other findings: Consideration of supply chain risks differs not only among weapon system managers but also between

67

weapon system and sustainment mangers; and managing supply chain risks is rare and if done at all, it is more likely to be done in acquisition than in sustainment.

One reason for the lack of a proactive approach to supply chain risk management was, as noted, the lack of tools for identifying supply chain risks. Using our findings and recommendations flowing from them, we turn next to examples of prototype SCRM maps to identify many supply chain risks, increase their visibility, and help manage them.

6. Developing Prototype Supply Chain Risk Management Maps

In previous chapters, we developed a composite supply chain risk-management process and discussed some specific ways that leading private enterprises proactively manage supply chain risks. One of these was the mapping of possible risks. In this chapter, we examine how the Air Force might manage its supply chain risks more proactively. We do so by demonstrating how the Air Force can build SCRM maps with existing data, and we begin the process of more proactively managing supply-chain risks. To do this, we borrow a best practice of Cisco discussed above: mapping supplier locations and risks associated with them. We recognize that some threats do not depend on location and may even be displaced to other sites by efforts to harden some sites. Nevertheless, we offer this analysis as a way to illustrate issues that enterprises may address to reduce the risks they confront.

To map suppliers, we use Google Maps because it is readily available at no cost. Using F-15 Bill of Material information, we link part numbers to contract numbers as well as to the supplier place of performance as listed in the FPDS. To link consumables to their place of performance, we used the AFMC Strategic Sourcing Analysis Tool for FYs 2004 to 2008 to link National Item Identification Number of the part to the contract number for it and then obtained corresponding information from the FPDS.

Figure 6.1 shows the location of active Air Force F-15 suppliers in the United States.[35] This provides a perspective of the supply base not currently available. The clustering of suppliers by geographic region provides a strategic view of the Air Force F-15 supply base.

The map also suggests the need for further exploration of the type of parts supplied and the weapon systems supported by these suppliers. We offer some such exploration in Figure 6.2, showing the location of suppliers of mission-critical parts for the F-15 (without which the aircraft cannot function as intended). This map shows a sample of such suppliers in Florida, California, Illinois, Connecticut, and Massachusetts.

---

[35] We plotted suppliers by ZIP code from the place of performance address found in the FPDS. The place of performance is the principal plant or place of business where the items will be produced or supplied from stock or where the service will be performed. It is not the headquarters or billing center of a supplier (unless those are co-located with the place of performance).

Figure 6.1. Air Force F-15 Suppliers Located Throughout the United States

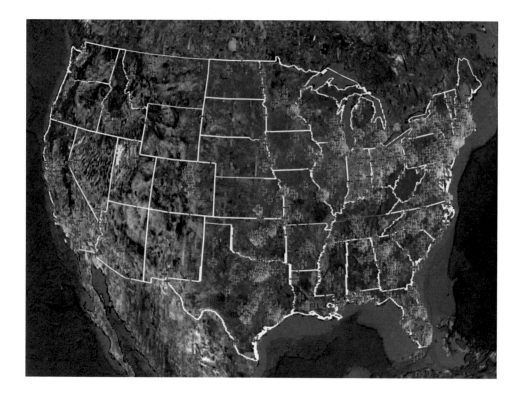

Other maps could yield additional insights on Air Force suppliers. For example, we might plot all suppliers that provide parts for the F-15 and for other Air Force weapon systems, using different colors to identify those providing parts to multiple weapon systems. Likewise, we could code suppliers to reflect the dollar value of the contracts held by each. We could also code new suppliers, those with quality problems, or still other supplier characteristics. This would permit the Air Force's weapon system managers to strategically manage relations with suppliers and prioritize those needing more watchful management.

One such additional characteristic supply chain managers may wish to map is exposure to natural disasters. Figure 6.3 overlays seismic hazards (specifically, earthquakes affecting an area since 1569) with the F-15 suppliers shown above. As noted above, earthquakes can uncover key weaknesses in SCRM; as an example, the March 2011 Japan earthquake caused many firms to realize that they did not know all their upstream suppliers and the effects these had on their operations. Still other maps could show suppliers by other risks such as those posed by financial performance, quality problems, or late delivery. Even in a state like California, not all regions are equally at

**Figure 6.2. Locations of a Sample of Suppliers for F-15
Mission-Critical Parts**

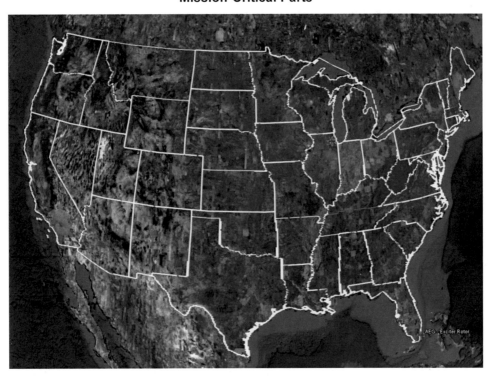

risk from major earthquakes. Managers may also be unaware of earthquake risks in regions such as the Midwest and the Southeast (although the only supplier shown in an earthquake-risk zone in Figure 6.3 does indeed appear to be in Southern California).

Figure 6.4 shows how, using a simple map pop-up, a weapon system manager might easily see more information on a supplier at risk and the part it provides. Such information might also be arranged to list suppliers within categories of interest. Managers might use such a map tactically, identifying, for example, suppliers by ZIP code area in a region of California suffering a major earthquake and assessing the likely consequences of the earthquake on the supply of parts. Although this may seem an obvious SCRM tactic, the Air Force does not currently have a way to quickly identify suppliers affected by events such as earthquakes.

Just as the Air Force could map suppliers by the risk earthquakes pose to them, so it could map suppliers by the risks each faces for another disaster such as a hurricane. Figure 6.5 shows F-15 suppliers in hurricane-risk zones. Not surprisingly, the two suppliers in Florida are at risk for hurricanes. The "pop-up" information also shows that Summit Aerospace, a company in the hurricane-risk zone, owns a proprietary method for repairing the Exciter Rotor produced by AEG Industrial Engineering. This part was in

**Figure 6.3. A Sample of Suppliers for F-15 Mission-Critical Parts
by Earthquake Risk**

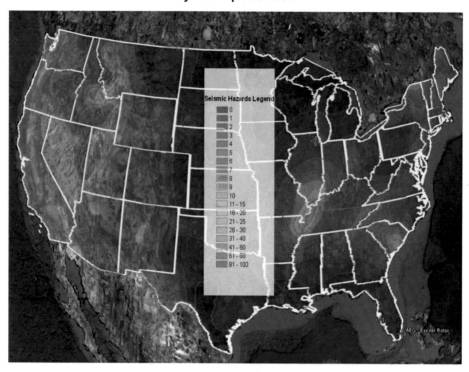

SOURCE: Seismic hazards data are from the *National Atlas of the United States* (2012).

short supply at the time of our research and was reducing mission-capability rates. Even if the supplier did not suffer damage in the event of a hurricane, power in the area could be lost for a week or more. Knowing that this supplier has a proprietary technology and is in a hurricane-risk zone could perhaps prompt business-continuity plans that included power backups.

Tornadoes may pose another risk as well. As Figure 6.6 shows, F-15 suppliers in Florida are at the greatest risk for tornadoes, with suppliers in California and parts of the northeast coast at some risk as well. Overlaying the maps of suppliers at risk for natural disasters would show that the sample of suppliers in Illinois, Connecticut, and Massachusetts are less likely to be affected by any natural disaster risks; this, too, is valuable information.

Still more detailed maps can help with response to ongoing events. In late 2009, a series of wildfires in California came perilously close to industrial zones. The U.S. Forest Service provided information on the spread of the fires, their speed and direction, and information on whether they were under control. We pulled this information onto Google Maps and plotted Air Force suppliers in the region (Figure 6.7). A simple plot like this can quickly allow mangers to identify suppliers at risk.

72

Figure 6.4. Identifying Characteristics of a Sample of Suppliers of F-15 Mission-Critical Parts in Earthquake-Risk Zones

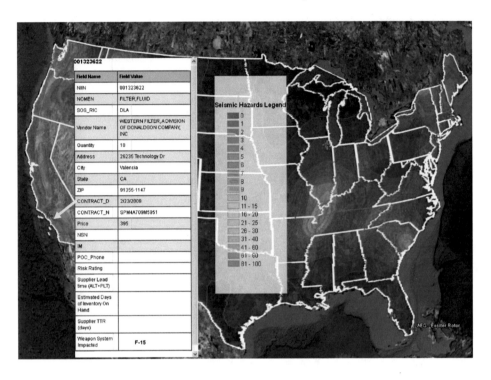

Figure 6.5. Identifying Characteristics of a Sample of Suppliers of F-15 Mission-Critical Parts in Hurricane-Risk Zones

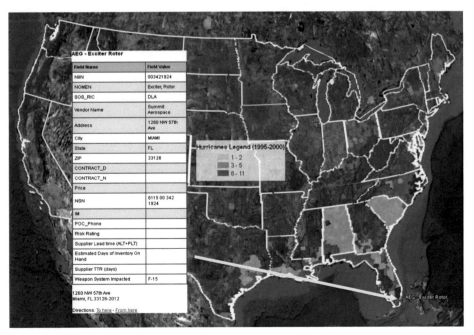

SOURCE: Hurricane data are from the *National Atlas of the United States* (2012).

**Figure 6.6. A Sample of Suppliers of F-15 Mission-Critical Parts
by Tornado Risk**

SOURCE: Tornado data are from the *National Atlas of the United States* (2012).

Spare-parts suppliers are not the only cause for concern. A failure in the supply of raw materials can increase costs and delay production. Figure 6.8 shows the locations of two titanium suppliers, Timet and RTI. We show their fabrication facilities in green and other facilities in yellow. We also show their proximity to earthquake-prone zones.

As the map indicates, Timet has a fabrication facility in the San Francisco area—one of the most earthquake-prone regions in the nation. Both companies also have other facilities in other earthquake-prone regions such as the Los Angeles area, southern Nevada, and even near the New Madrid fault in the central United States.

Figure 6.9 shows that RTI has fabrication facilities in high-risk hurricane zones, particularly the Houston area. Knowing the output of material from locations at high risk for earthquakes, hurricanes, or other natural disasters, and the effect on supply from even a temporary closure, could help encourage development of appropriate SCRM plans.

Figure 6.7. Recent Fires and Air Force Suppliers in Southern California

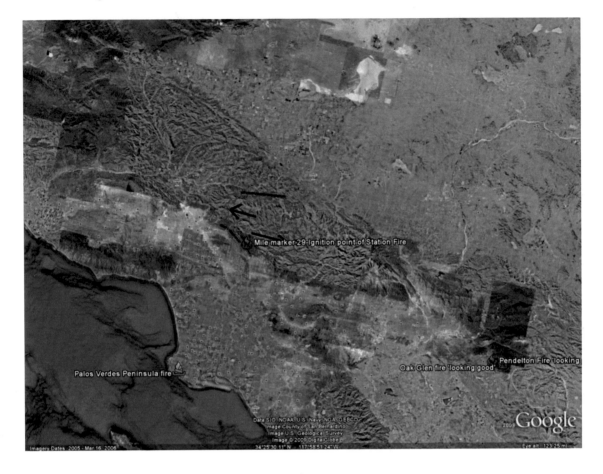

Figure 6.8. Potential Risks Posed by Earthquakes to Upstream Titanium Suppliers

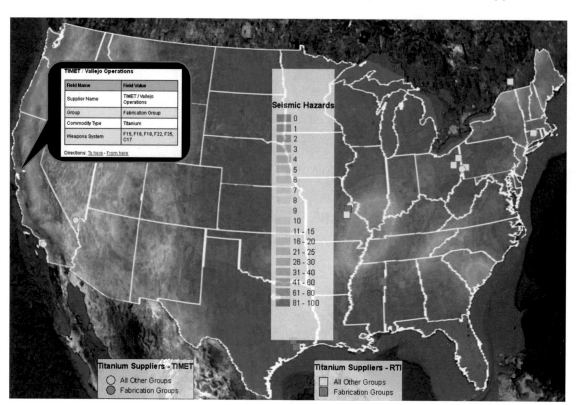

Figure 6.9. Potential Risks Posed by Hurricanes to Upstream Titanium Suppliers

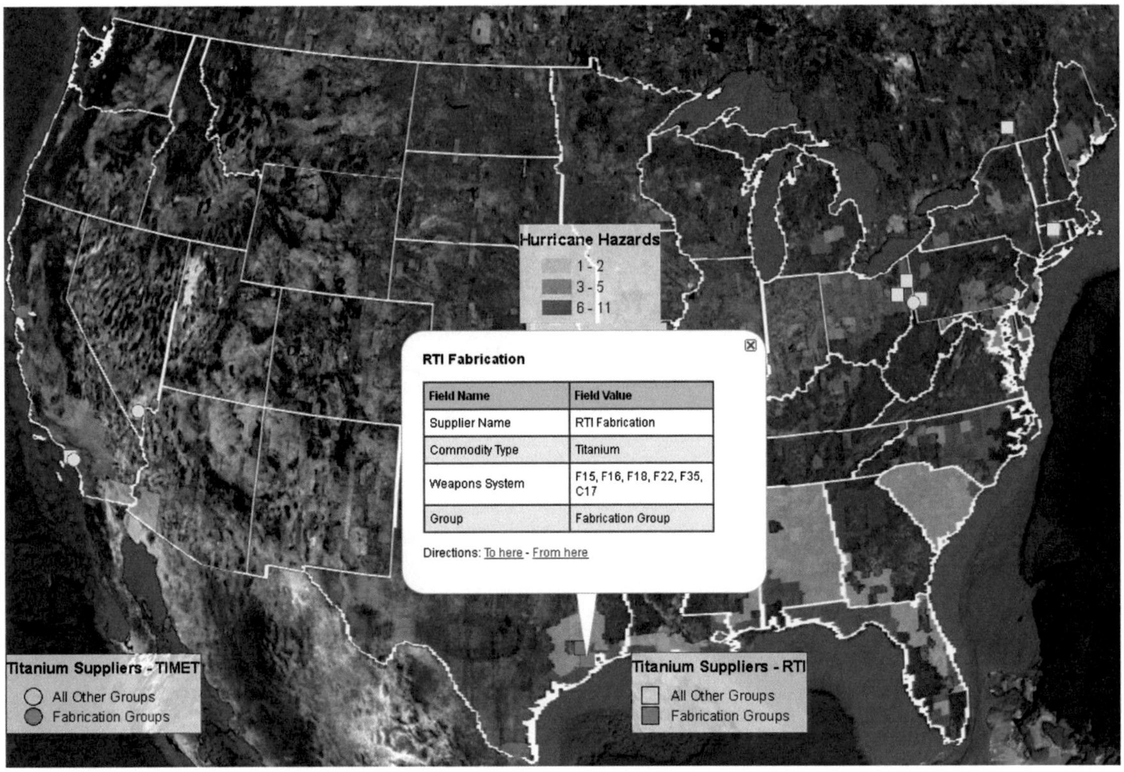

7. Conclusions and Recommendations

This analysis revealed many opportunities for DoD and the Air Force to strengthen the management of supply chain risks. However, although DoD and the Air Force provide some guidance related to supply chain risks, it does not incorporate many of the supply chain risks identified in the best practice literature. We also did not identify a comprehensive SCRM process for the F-16, suggesting that Air Force organic weapon support may more generally lack this kind of management. Boeing management of C-17 sustainment has some SCRM elements emerging from its corporate supply chain management policy, but it was not clear whether this was used to identify supply chain risks beyond those relating to finances, quality, or timeliness. Air Force commodity councils have a process for managing supply chain risk, but it is geared toward contract risk. Nevertheless, this process could expand to focus on supply chain risk as part of a broader supplier-relationship management policy. The shift to PBL has been transferring sustainment management, including SCRM, to suppliers.

The best practice structures that we found for managing supply chain risks varied. The companies that had a more clearly defined supply chain risk program also had small organizations (four or five personnel) that helped coordinate SCRM activities across business units and at levels extending to corporate headquarters.

We envision a similar organization for the Air Force, perhaps located within AFMC or the Air Staff. This organization would provide SCRM policy and guidance to program executive officers and the Air Force Sustainment Center to help proactively manage their SCRs. It would also monitor and help policymakers react to supply chain risks at an enterprise level, both strategically and tactically. It would help ensure that sustainment is considered early in the defense acquisition system, either in advice to the Senior Acquisition Executive (SAE) or developing SAE policies. The role and scope of this organization would need to be clearly defined, but it would provide an enterprise view of supply chain risks and help mitigate risks across weapon systems. Specifically, this organization would

- set policy on how to manage supply chain risk under both organic and contractor-managed sustainment
- develop standard processes and metrics for risk management, including setting expectations for business continuity plans and time-to-recovery metrics
- expand the types of risks managed
- develop tools for risk assessment, including, for example, sense-and-respond processes to monitor disruptions and initiate contingency plans

- provide effective training in risk identification, assessment, and management
- establish metrics and incentives.

Our findings point to two key recommendations with a number of actionable steps.

First, we recommend that the Air Force develop tools to help identify, assess, and manage supply chain risks based on leading industry practices. Air Force personnel do not currently have the visibility and assessment tools they need to adequately identify, assess, and manage supply chain risks. For example, the Air Force could quickly build prototype supply chain risk maps similar to the ones Cisco developed and we adapted to Air Force data to help personnel identify and manage supply chain risks. Because SCRM is an emerging best practice, the Air Force could collaborate with and leverage companies with more mature SCRM programs to adapt and adopt prototype SCRM tools to best meet its own needs. One organization for doing this is the SCRLC, which published a compilation of SCRM best practices and developed a supply chain risk management maturity model (SCRLC, 2011 and 2013). The Air Force can use these best practices and the SCRM maturity model as a foundation for developing its own SCRM practices, processes, and organizations.

Second, we recommend that the Air Force refine existing policy and develop new policies and processes to identify, measure, assess, and manage supply chain risks across weapon systems and over their life cycles. Current policies and processes related to SCRM during acquisition and sustainment are inadequate. SCRM policy and training should be expanded and standardized to provide personnel with the direction and capabilities to better understand and manage supply chain risks throughout the stages of weapon system design, manufacturing, and sustainment. It should also help personnel identify the types of supply chain risks that they should focus on managing and provide incentives for managing them. SCRM ought to be elevated within the weapon system acquisition process, so that it is linked to, but not overshadowed by, cost, schedule, and technology issues. It should also be better linked to technology development and manufacturing risks, which do get attention. Last, SCRM must flow up the supply chain from prime contractors to their suppliers and their suppliers' suppliers. Some of the most critical supply chain risks may exist several levels upstream where they have been invisible to the Air Force. Pushing SCRM up the supply chain increases awareness, assessment, and management.

Currently, shorter-term manufacturing cost, schedule, and technology risks compete for attention with longer-term sustainment supply chain cost, schedule, and technology risks, and, usually, shorter-term manufacturing risks receive higher priority. The incentives and tenure of weapon system acquisition personnel lead them to focus on solving current problems and containing damage from them rather than trying to avoid or minimize longer-term disruptions and reduce total life-cycle costs. Indeed, often personnel will have moved to other jobs or retired before longer-term supply chain risks are realized.

Longer-term SCRM requires equal priority with shorter-term cost, schedule, and technology issues. The visibility of short- and long-term SCRM should be equalized relative to the factors they affect, such as cost, and the incentives to address both should be aligned in the acquisition process.

The design phase offers the greatest opportunity for proactively managing supply chain risks such as promoting standardization and commonality, specifying subsystems and suppliers, minimizing obsolescence, and elevating the visibility of supply chain risks and costs to the MDA. The longer SCRM is delayed in the weapon system life cycle, the fewer options and leverage will be available for proactive management. Delaying SCRM can mean forgoing such options as signing a sustainment contract at the same time the production contract is signed or strategically managing suppliers enterprise-wide.

One way to align incentives during the acquisition process is to create parallel short- and long-term weapon system teams, risk matrices, and reporting. Short-term risk management would focus on reactive damage control, and long-term risk management would focus on proactive minimization. Having separate teams produce short- and long-term risk matrices and report them at major milestones will help longer-term risks avoid being overshadowed or given lower priority in planning than more immediate risks receive. Figure 7.1 illustrates how parallel risk matrices could be illustrated during the weapon system acquisition process.

Figure 7.1. Parallel Short- and Long-Term Weapon System Risk Matrices

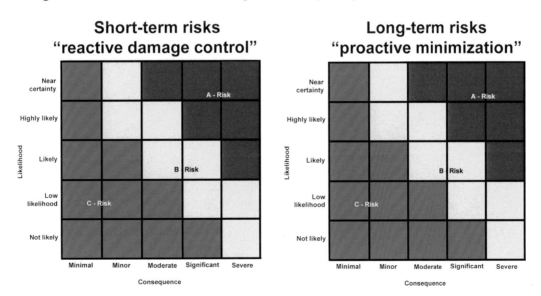

SOURCE: Payton (2008).

81

Because the Air Force does not make its own weapons, it must ensure that their manufacturers adopt an SCRM program. It can do so by incorporating SCRM into production and life-cycle support contracts such as PBL and other logistics-support contracts. Contracts may include requirements for business-continuity plans and commitments to recovery times in the event of disruption. Many manufacturers have become assemblers of major subassemblies, with most production and, hence, costs shifted to upstream suppliers. Consequently, requirements for business-continuity plans and recovery times ought to flow up the supply base. New requirements for subaward reporting should help the Air Force learn more about its upstream supply base.

We also recommend that the Air Force incorporate SCRM into its supplier relationship management (to include interactions with external and DoD suppliers, e.g., DLA) processes and practices and adopt best practices in purchasing and supply management and supplier relationship management, without which best SCRM practices are extremely difficult to follow.

For its most pressing supply chain risks, the Air Force should start developing mitigation plans that it can use as templates for broader implementation. It must also start mapping its upstream suppliers, locations, and the parts and weapons they support. Last, it should monitor disruptions and quickly implement contingency plans for those suppliers, parts, and the weapons they affect.

Successful adoption of best SCRM practices often involves changing the culture as well as the processes of all key stakeholders in the extended supply chain. Changing an organization's culture is an evolutionary process that requires a well-designed plan and strong support from senior leaders. We offer this research as a means for the Air Force to continue the cultural changes it has begun to improve its SCRM practices.

A. Interview Protocol for F-16, C-17, and DLA Interviews

RAND Project AIR FORCE
Identifying and Managing Risks Associated with Agile Supply Chains
Sponsored by: AF/A4/7, AF/A4I

Background

RAND is conducting an analysis, entitled *Identifying and Managing Risks Associated with Agile Supply Chains*, sponsored by the Air Force Director of Transformation within Logistics, Installations & Mission Support. Its objective is to assist the Air Force with development of an enterprise-wide strategy for proactively managing sustainment support supply chain risks across the Air Force's portfolio of weapon systems. The current study seeks to identify important weapon system sustainment supply chain risks the Air Force is managing, those it is not managing, and those it should manage for legacy or near-legacy systems.

The result of this RAND effort will be a briefing and RAND report. We do not intend to identify anyone we interview in our briefing or report other than general offices or industries. If we receive any figures or tables during our interviews that we would like to use in our reports, we will seek permission to use them and guidance on how to properly acknowledge the source.

BACKGROUND

1. What is the role of your office in the Air Force weapon system sustainment support supply chain?

2. For respondents supporting weapon system sustainment, please describe your supply chain, including

    a. The part(s) or system(s) you manage

    b. Your major upstream suppliers for 2.a.

        i. The major suppliers to these suppliers

    c. Your major downstream customers for 2.a.

        i. Customers of your major customers, if applicable

    d. The annual volume managed including quantity and value by source of supply

    e. Number of single source suppliers

    f. Number of Diminished Manufacturing Source (DMS)[36] suppliers

TYPES OF SUSTAINMENT SUPPLY CHAIN RISKS

3. The attached table presents many typical types of risks associated with managing different types of supply chains in the commercial sector.

    a. Which of these risks are actively managed by your office (or by another office that you can provide)?

    b. Are there risks that your office manages that are not represented in the table?

4. For each of the risks identified in question 1, can you provide

    a. Air Force policy, directive, or other documentation about how the risk is or should be managed

    b. Data and/or analyses used in the assessment of that risk, its likelihood, duration, and impact on your sustainment supply chain

    c. Data and/or analyses of the ranking of the importance of the risk to the Air Force based on its likelihood of occurrence, duration, and impact

    d. Plans for avoidance, mitigation, or management of that risk, its frequency and actual impact on your supply chain

---

[36] According to DoD 4140.1-R, *DoD Supply Chain Materiel Management Regulation*, diminishing manufacturing sources and material shortages (DMSMS) is "the loss or impending loss of manufacturers of items or suppliers of items or raw materials may cause material shortages that endanger a weapon system's or equipment's development, production, or post-production support capability." DMSMS directly affects system readiness and system availability and costs DoD hundreds of millions of dollars annually.

Typical Supply Chain Risks	Does This Apply to the Air Force?	Is There a Plan to Prevent?	Plan ID	Date	Is There a Plan to Mitigate?	Plan ID	Date
Shortage of supply							
- Quality defects in manufactured product							
- Diminishing source of manufacturing - Unplanned demand exceeds production/ repair/transportation capacity							
- Price fluctuations							
Environmental: Natural or man made disasters							
- Distribution disruptions							
- Transportation network compromised							
- Existing warehouse inaccessible							
- Production/repair capacity diminished							
- IT structure compromised - Business sector shows signs of weakening (i.e., supplier failures on the rise)							
Structural							
- Single source suppliers							
- Diminishing manufacturing source suppliers							
- No technical drawings							
Funding - Underfunding supply requirements							
Other Risks							

5. For each risks you did *not* identify as actively managing in question 2:

   a. Are you aware of any of the risks applying to your sustainment supply chain or to other Air Force or DoD sustainment supply chains? If so, can you tell us or point us to where we can learn what happened, when did it happen, and what was the duration and impact, and what was done to shorten its duration?

   b. Could any other risks apply to your sustainment supply chain?

      i. Yes/No?

      ii. If yes, how would it be managed? (see question 2)

6. Using the attached graphic, the answer from 2.b., and the professional guidelines you use to perform your duties, which risks are most important to the AF and why are they important?

   a. Of these, what do you think is the likelihood of the risk to your sustainment supply chain?

      i. What is the likelihood of the risk to other Air Force or DoD sustainment supply chains?

   b. What do you think would be the impact of the risk to your sustainment supply chain?

ii. What is the impact of the risk to other Air Force or DoD sustainment supply chains?

PARTNERS IN SUSTAINMENT SUPPLY CHAIN RISKS

7. Which, if any, of the sustainment supply chain risks that you manage are affected by decisions made by someone else either earlier in the weapon system acquisition process or elsewhere in the sustainment supply chain?

    a. What were the decisions and how have they affected the risks you manage (e.g., the risk's likelihood, duration, or impact or limited risk avoidance, mitigation, or contingency actions)?

    b. Are the risks that you manage in your sustainment supply chain affected by decisions or actions in the sustainment supply chain for other weapon systems [i.e., not the C-17 or F-16]?

8. What should we know about identifying, assessing, prioritizing, and managing sustainment supply chain risks in the Air Force that we have not asked you?

    a. Who else would you recommend we talk to about sustainment supply chain risks for your weapon system?

    b. Can you point us to data, tool, or Air Force and DoD literature to help us better understand how the Air Force is identifying, assessing, prioritizing, and managing its sustainment supply chains?

B. Supply Chain Risks That We Asked Sustainment and Acquisition Personnel If They Considered

This table lists all the risks that we asked sustainment and acquisition personnel if they considered. Personnel were asked to rank the frequency with which they considered each risk. The results of their responses are presented in the body of this document.

Type of Risk Frequency with which you consider this risk 1=never, 2=rarely, 3=half time, 4=often, 5=always

ENVIRONMENTAL RISK

Natural Disasters
Weather
Hurricanes
Tornados/cyclones
Blizzards/hailstorms/lightning
Floods/mudslides
Droughts
Earthquakes
Tsunamis
Volcanoes
Rogue waves
Epidemics
Infestations

Terrorism/Sabotage
Bombings
Chemical/biological release
Blockades
Product tampering
Electronic intrusions
Viruses
Worms
Trojan horses
Denial of service
Property theft
  – Physical
  – Intellectual

Business Environment
Government actions
  – Taxes/tariffs
  – Regulations

– Customs

– Currency devaluations

Lawsuits

– Environmental

– Health and safety

– Intellectual property

Economic recessions/depressions

Labor

– Availability/shortages

– Quality

– Cost

– Unrest

Strikes

Work slowdowns

Political unrest/instability

– Boycotts

Market Environment

Capacity constraints

Unstable prices

Uncertain currency rates

Little or no competition

Entry barriers

Capital requirements

Specific assets

Proprietary (i.e., patents)

– Design

– Processes

Low profitability

Certification/qualification

Raw materials

Availability

Cost trends

Geographic concentration of suppliers

Acts of War

Bombings

Blockades

Accidents

Fires

Explosions

Structural failures

Hazardous spills

Technological Uncertainty

Overall availability

Obsolescence

Pace of change

Direction of change

DEMAND UNCERTAINTY/VOLATILITY

Surges

Shortfalls

– Expedite jobs

– Poor customer requirements/specifications

– Product configuration changes

Changes in fleet life cycle (longer or shorter)

SUPPLIER RISKS

Bankruptcy/financial failure

Withdrawal from the market

Inability to sustain during a downturn

– Utilize slack

– Reserve funds

Inadequate contingency/risk management planning

Poor quality/rework

– Failure to maintain equipment

– Lack of training/knowledge in principles and techniques

Constrained volume capacity

– Equipment, personnel, or facilities

Excess capacity

– Equipment, personnel, or facilities

Inflexible mix (i.e., production) capability

Shortage of inputs (materials and services)

– Poor forecasting

– Long and/or variable purchasing cycle times

Long lead/order cycle times—unresponsive

– Backlogs

Variable lead/order cycle times—unreliable

Inability to control/reduce costs

Unwillingness/inability to continually improve

High management/personnel turnover

Slow adoption of technological changes

Incompatible information systems

Dependency on buyer, one, or a few large customers

Intellectual property theft

Critical technology disclosure (i.e., ITAR)

Downstream integration/direct competition

Substituting harmful/inferior/patent violating materials or parts

Illegal/poor labor/environmental practices

Poor quality internal and external information flow

Inflating purchase costs

Opaque processes

Practices that threaten viability of key upstream suppliers

Opportunistic behavior

Security requirements/clearance for facilities/personnel

Certification (e.g., FAA)

Transition to new supplier (time, cost, quality)

INBOUND AND OUTBOUND DIST

Constraints

Infrastructure

– Ports

– Roads

– Rail

– Air

Asset

– Cargo aircraft

– Container ships

– Locomotives/rail cars

– Chassis

– Containers

Labor

– Truck drivers

– Rail operators

– Longshoremen

– Pilots

Long Distances

Longer lead times

Increased chance of disruption

Damage in transit

Many Touch Points

Security

– Theft

– Terrorism/tampering

Damage in transit

– Increased costs

– Incompatible information technology

INTERNAL RISKS

Personnel

– Numbers and experience

– Knowledge and skills

Design

– Lack of tech drawings/verification (product model/configuration) modifications

– Complexity

– Validity of data

Manufacturability

Value to the enterprise

– Effect on customer satisfaction/loyalty

– Effect on liability

– Effect on costs/profits

Value to Final Product/Application

– Customer demand

– Uniqueness

– Substitutability

– Systems integration

Availability of organic facilities

Plant breakdowns/mechanical failures

Reliability of test equipment

Inventory obsolescence

Forecast reliability/ schedule availability

Knowledge of supplier costs

DCMA availability

Work scope/plan creep

Competition/bid process

Poor communication

– Suppliers

– Customers

Acquisition strategy

Program maturity

Integration testing

Flight test

– Qualifications

– Schedule

Funding availability

Subcontracting agreement

C. Interview Protocol for Company Interviews

SCRM Company Interview Protocol

Background

RAND, a non-profit corporation dedicated to objective analysis of important public policy questions, was asked by the U.S. Air Force to assess its ability to identify, evaluate, manage, and mitigate weapon system support supply chain risk. As part of this study, we are studying best commercial practices for supply chain risk management to learn the latest trends and corporate strategies for managing them. We are also interviewing Air Force personnel regarding how they identify supply chain risk, who is responsible for assessing and managing this risk, and how they mitigate supply chain risk.

RAND would like to understand how your company approaches supply chain risk management. Our project is particularly concerned with aftermarket supply chain risk.

Questions on Risk Management

1. How did your company's approach to supply chain risk management change after 9/11? Were there other events that had an impact on your company's perception of supply chain risk management?

2. Which corporate areas conduct supply chain risk assessments (i.e., manufacturing, supplier relations, etc.)?

3. How are supply chain risk assessments and risk management strategies communicated throughout the enterprise? How often?

4. Is there a single organization for managing supply chain risks? Where does this organization fit in the org chart?

5. How is supply chain risk management organized?

   a. What type of experience and skills are required by your company to work in supply chain risk management?

   b. Are employees working in the supply chain risk organization promoted to other units within your company, or is this seen as a career position?

   c. What is the average tenure of someone working in this area?

   d. How many employees are directly involved in management of supply chain risk?

   e. Are these employees fully dedicated to this function or do they share their risk responsibility with other tasks?

93

     f.   What is the function of the supply chain risk management organization, i.e., does it facilitate, oversee, audit, or control supply chain risk management at your company?

6.   How often is supply chain risk assessed? Does this vary by commodity or product?

7.   Does your company have a written process for conducting supply chain risk assessments?

8.   When assessing a supplier, what types of risks is your company concerned with?

9.   Does your company start assessing supply chain risk during the product design phase? If so when in product design?

10.   Once a product moves from prototype development to production is there a change in the responsibility for management supply chain risk?

11.   Is the board of directors briefed on supply chain risk?

D. Interview Protocol for Personnel Responsible for Acquisition Issues

RAND PROJECT AIR FORCE
IMPROVING SUSTAINMENT PLANNING IN ACQUISITION PROGRAMS TO REDUCE LIFE CYCLE COSTS AND MITIGATE SUPPLY CHAIN RISKS
Sponsored by: AF/A4I

Background

RAND is conducting a study, entitled *Improving Sustainment Planning in Acquisition Programs to Reduce Life Cycle Costs and Mitigate Supply Chain Risks* which is co-sponsored by the Air Force Director of Transformation within Logistics, Installations & Mission Support and Deputy Assistant Secretary Acquisition Integration. Its objective is to assist the Air Force with planning for supply chain risks during the acquisition phase of new systems, with the goal of reducing total life cycle costs and avoiding or mitigating future sustainment supply chain risks. This includes identifying short- and long-term supply chain risks that the Air Force manages, those that are not managed, and those that should be managed.

The result of this RAND effort will be a briefing and RAND report. We do not intend to identify anyone we interview in our briefing or report other than general offices or industries. If we receive any figures or tables during our interviews that we would like to use in our reports, we will seek permission to use them and guidance on how to properly acknowledge the source.

We selected you for this interview because of your experience in the weapon system acquisition process.

Background. In this section we want some general background about the weapon system and the acquisition program.

1. What weapon system programs have you worked in?
   a. What acquisition categories were these in?
   b. What is the overall risk scores of these programs?

2. Do you have someone in your office who is an expert in sustainment supply chain issues during acquisition? If yes, who?

3. Briefly, what have been your roles or your experience in the acquisition process?

Supply Chain. In this section we want to learn about supply chain risks during acquisition.

4. Below is a list of supply chain risks that we have compiled from several sources. They are organized into four categories. In your experience, which of the following supply chain risks are considered during acquisition?

TYPE OF RISK	CONSIDERED
External Risks	
Natural Disasters	
Accidents	
Sabotage, Terrorism, Crime, and War	
Government Compliance and Political Uncertainty	
Labor Unavailability and Lack of Skill	
Market Challenges	
Lawsuits	
Technological Uncertainty	
Supplier Risks: External, DLA, Organic	
Physical and Regulatory Risks	
Key Suppliers Located in High Risk Areas	
Material Unavailability/Lack of Planning	
Legal Noncompliance	
Regulatory Noncompliance	
Production Problems	
Lack of Capacity	
Inflexible Production Capabilities	
Technological Inadequacies or Failures	
Poor Quality	
Financial/Cost Losses	
Competitive Pressures	
Financial Viability	
Management Risks	
Management Quality	
Lack of Continuous Improvement	
Lead Times	
Dependence on One or a Few Customer(s)	
Poor Communication	
Dishonesty (substituting inferior or illegal materials or parts)	
Inadequate Risk Management Planning	
Upstream Supply Risks	
Any of the Above	
Lower Tier Supplier Relationships	
Shrinking Number of Suppliers	

Transition Time and Costs for New Suppliers	
Distribution Risks: Inbound or Outbound	
Infrastructure Unavailability	
Vehicle Accidents/Lack of Capacity	
Labor Unrest/Unavailability	
Cargo Damage/Theft/Tampering	
Warehouse Unavailability/Insecurity	
IT System Inadequacies/Failures	
Long, Multi-Party Supply Pipelines	
Buying Enterprise Risks	
Demand Volatility	
Personnel Unavailability/Lack of Skill	
Design Uncertainty	
Planning Failures	
Financial Uncertainty/Losses	
Facility Unavailability/Unreliability	
Testing Unavailability/Inferiority	
Enterprise Underperformance/Lack of Value	
Inventory Obsolescence	
Use of Best Practices in Supplier Relationship Management	
Other Risks (Please specify)	

5. In which of the following phases of the acquisition process do you have experience?
    a. Concept Refinement Leading to Milestone A
    b. Technology Development Leading to Milestone B
    c. Supportability/Logistics Considerations in System Development Demonstration
    d. Supportability/Logistics Considerations in Production and Deployment
    e. Other

6. The table below lists major acquisition activities from the DoD Acquisition Guidebook, which may require logistics and supportability considerations. For the phases where you have worked, please indicate whether supply chain risks of the kind listed above were ever considered and, if so, how often.

    For those stages where respondent checks anything other than "Never," ask the following:

    a. Which risks were considered here? You may want to go back to the list in Question 4.
    b. How important were these risks? How did you decide their importance?
    c. Did you take any mitigation steps? If yes, please describe. If no, why not?

HOW OFTEN CONSIDERED ACQUISITION STAGE	Never	Rarely	Half the Time	Often	Always
Concept Refinement Leading to Milestone A					
Entry Documents:					
Initial Capabilities Document					
Analysis of Alternatives Plan					
Exit Documents/Activities:					
Analysis of Alternatives					
Technology Development Strategy					
Consideration of Technology Issues					
Test and Evaluation Strategy					
Technology Development Leading to Milestone B					
Entry Documents:					
Analysis of Alternatives					
Technology Development Strategy					
Market Analysis					
Consideration of Technology Issues					
Test and Evaluation Strategy					
Exit Documents/Activities:					
Analysis of Alternatives					
Technology Development Strategy					
Initial Capabilities Document and Capability Development Document					
Technology Readiness Assessment					
Information Support Plan					
Acquisition Strategy					
Industrial Capabilities					
Core Logistics Analysis/Source of Repair Analysis					
Competition Analysis for Depot-Level Maintenance >$3M					
Cooperative Opportunities					
Test and Evaluation Master Plan (TEMP)					
Live-Fire Waiver and Alternative LFT&E Plan					
Operational Test Agency Report of OT&E Results					
Independent Cost Estimate and Manpower Estimate					
Affordability Assessment					
DoD Component Cost Analysis					
Acquisition Program Baseline (APB)					
Supportability/Logistics Consideration in System Development & Demonstration					
Entry Documents (System Integration):					
Initial Capabilities Document and Capability Development Document					
Acquisition Strategy					
Technology Development Strategy					
Acquisition Program Baseline					
Entry Documents (System Demonstration):					
Design Readiness Review					
Developmental Test and Evaluation Report					
Operational Test Plan					

HOW OFTEN CONSIDERED / ACQUISITION STAGE	Never	Rarely	Half the Time	Often	Always
Exit Documents/Activities:					
Update Documents from MS B as Appropriate					
Capability Production Document					
Supportability/Logistics Consideration in Production & Deployment					
Entry Documents:					
Capability Development Document, Capability Production Document					
Exit Documents/Activities:					
Update Documents from MS C as Appropriate					
LFT&E Report					
DoD Component LFT&E Report					
Information Supportability Certification					
Post Deployment Review					
Other Processes					
Design Reviews					
Program Management Reviews					
Risk Working Group					
Configuration Control Boards					
Production Readiness Reviews					
ILS Reviews/Working Groups					

7.   A Total System Product Support Package (TSPSP) identifies support issues. (Section 5.2.2). In day-to-day acquisition activities, how often are the following TSPSP issues considered, in your experience.

> For those stages where respondent checks anything other than "Never," ask the following:
>
> a.   Which risks were considered here? You may want to go back to the list in Question 4.
>
> b.   How important were these risks? Do any fall in the "A" category of the ABC 5x5 table? How did you decide their importance?
>
> c.   Did you take any mitigation steps? If yes, please describe. If no, why not?

TSPSP Issues / How Often Considered	Never	Rarely	Half the Time	Often	Always
Supply Support (Spare/Repair Parts)					
Maintenance Planning					
Test/Support Equipment					
Technical Documentation/Interactive Electronic Technical Manuals					
Manpower & Training/Computer Based Training					
Facilities					
Packaging Handling Storage & Transportation					
Design Interface/Computing Support					

8. In your experience, do the criteria specified for source selection include any of the supply chain risks discussed above in Question 4? If yes, which ones?

9. Is your weapon system's OEM required to have a business continuity plan?
    a. If so, what kind of risks do you require in the plan?
    b. How often do you review the plan?

10. Do the subcontracting plans submitted by OEMs address supply chain risks among subcontractors?
    a. If so, what risks does it address?

11. Does your office get insight into your prime contractors or into their subcontractors from onsite interactions?
    a. How about through DCMA surveillance?
    b. What kind of insight do you get? Does any of it relate to supply chain risk?

12. In your experience, have you ever seen short-term supply chain risks (i.e., risks during production) or long-term supply chain risks (i.e., risks during sustainment) affecting an acquisition decision?
    a. If so, please describe.
    b. Did this experience with a supply chain risk shape future risk assessments?

Closing

13. Are there other important supply chain risks that that your weapon system office is not able to capture? If so, can you describe these?

14. What Air Force policy or DoD guidance have you used the most for managing risk?

15. Could we get a copy of a risk management plan created by your office?
    a. Do you normally include both short-term (i.e., production) and long-term (i.e., sustainment) supply chain risks in your risk management plans?

16. Could we also get a copy of:
    a. The contract, or relevant sections of it
    b. KPPs/KPIs
    c. Production Readiness Review

17. Who else should we contact regarding to supply chain risk considerations during acquisition?

18. Is there anything else we haven't asked about managing risks that we should be aware of?
    a. Are there particular impediments to managing risk that we haven't asked about?

19. Please take the attached list and mark which, if any, risks are actively considered during acquisition. [See Appendix B for list.]

E. Description of DoD and Air Force Guidance on Acquisition and Supply Chain Risk

Defense Acquisition Guidebook **(Defense Acquisition University, 2013)**

The *Defense Acquisition Guidebook* is a reference document to help acquisition professionals understand and apply the material in DoD Directive 5000.01 and DoD Instruction 5000.2. The section most relevant to supply chain risk management is in Chapter 4 of the handbook. Below, we briefly describe the chapters.

A.   Chapter 1, "Department of Defense Decision Support Systems"

This chapter describes the context of acquisition at the Department of Defense. It looks specifically at the Planning, Programming, Budgeting, and Execution process for setting up an acquisition; at the Joint Capabilities Integration and Development System regarding needs; and at the Defense Acquisition System regarding procurement.

B.   Chapter 2, "Defense Acquisition Program Goals and Strategy"

This chapter describes the purpose and process of formulating goals for acquisition, looking at the Joint Capabilities Integration, the Technology Development Strategy, and the Acquisition Strategy as stages of that process.

C.   Chapter 3, "Affordability and Life-Cycle Resource Estimates"

This chapter describes how to determine affordability over the life cycle of an acquisition program and how to satisfy DoD policy requirements in estimating and reporting those estimates of affordability.

D.   Chapter 4: "Systems Engineering"

This chapter explains systems engineering procedures and how to use them in the acquisition process. It examines questions of system design and gives direction for carrying out a Systems Engineering Plan. In discussing how systems engineering is implemented, section 4.2.3.5, "Risk Management," describes the requirements and process of risk management in acquisitions.

E.   Chapter 5: "Life-Cycle Logistics"

This chapter describes life-cycle logistics (LCL) and how it operates within the processes of acquisition and sustainment. It discusses how LCL operates within systems engineering to improve reliability and to lower the "logistics footprint," places priority on the use of PBL for product support, and describes the essential LCL activities in all the phases of a weapons system life cycle.

F.   Chapter 6: "Human Systems Integration (HSI)"

This chapter focuses on how best to use personnel resources in the acquisition process. It discusses each area of HSI: manpower, personnel, training, human factors, safety and occupational health, personnel survivability, and habitability.

G.   Chapter 7: "Acquiring Information Technology and National Security Systems"

This chapter describes the "network-centric strategy" used by DoD, examining the Global Information Grid (GIG), how to make programs operable across the GIG, how to make data accessible and useful (including across the electromagnetic spectrum), and how and when to use commercial solutions to achieve these goals.

H.   Chapter 8: "Intelligence, Counterintelligence, and Security Support"

This chapter examines the unintended loss of military technology and strategy through "inadvertent technology transfer." It describes prevention and protection strategies.

I.   Chapter 9: "Integrated Test and Evaluation"

This chapter addresses the T&E phase. It describes how to develop a T&E strategy that will provide necessary information for furthering the acquisition process.

J.   Chapter 10: "Decisions, Assessments, and Periodic Reporting"

This chapter describes the time line of decisions and reviews for which program managers are responsible.

K.   Chapter 11: "Program Management Activities"

This chapter describes the major management actions for which program managers are responsible. These include

1.   joint programs
2.   international cooperation
3.   integrated program management

4. earned value management

5. contract management reporting

6. risk management

7. knowledge-based acquisition

8. performance-based business environment

9. total life cycle systems management

10. integrated product and process development

11. technical representatives at contractor facilities

12. contractor councils

13. government property in the possession of contractors

14. integrated digital environment

15. simulation-based acquisition and modeling and simulation

16. independent expert review of software-intensive programs.

Risk Management Guide for DoD Acquisition (Department of Defense, 2006)

This guide gives specific directions for managing risk to program managers. It defines a risk event as having three distinct elements: a future root cause, the probability of that cause occurring, and the consequence or duration of the event. The guide emphasizes plans for risk mitigation and implementing those plans rather than simply relying on strategies to avoid risk. This is especially evident in its emphasis on future root causes. By describing how the chance of a risk occurring depends on the chance of the root cause, the focus shifts from simple attempts to minimize effects to more comprehensive efforts to understand and avoid the causes. The guide distinguishes between managing risks and issues: Risks are future events with future consequences, whereas issues are current problems. Risk management thus involves mitigating possible future events, not solving current problems.

Acquisition and Sustainment Life Cycle Management (Air Force Instruction 63-101, 2009)

This document establishes the integrated life-cycle management guidelines, policies, and procedures to be applied by Air Force personnel in managing systems and subsystems procured under DoD's 5000.2 series directive. Although this document does not mention sustainment risk explicitly, it lays out a requirement to manage and measure program life-cycle performance. This document attempts to integrate the acquisition and sustainment early in the life cycle of a program. Section 3.13 discusses the need to establish metrics to measure sustainment performance but gives no specific direction on assessing supply chain risk.

DoD Supply Chain Materiel Management Regulation (DoDI 4140.1-R, Office of the Deputy Under Secretary of Defense for Logistics and Materiel Readiness, 2003)

This guide provides the required procedures for managing DoD materiel. It defines and describes the supply chain, planning for materiel, the sourcing and acquisition of materiel, materiel production and maintenance, materiel delivery and return, technology that supports these processes, and logistics programs and systems that support these processes. It addresses but does not discuss in any detail the following risks: the proximate causes for the risk of an item being out of stock, draw-down of the stockpile, reducing the risk of shelf-life expiration, financial risks that may be associated with life-cycle support, exceeding repair cycle time, exceeding order and shipping time, exceeding the maintenance replacement rate, resupply from external sources, and security risks associated with particular weapons system categories.

USAF Deficiency Reporting, Investigation, and Resolution (TO-00-35D-54; Secretary of the Air Force, 2011)

This technical order implements the guidance of AFI 63-501, *The Air Force Acquisition Quality Program*. Its purpose is to establish product deficiency reporting procedures that will allow the Air Force to track and correct product quality deficiencies before they adversely affect operational safety, suitability, and effectiveness (OSS&E). Table 1.1 of the technical order lists attributes that may affect OSS&E, including quality, reliability, maintainability, and logistics supportability. The deficiency reporting information system is a repository of deficiency reports that could be mined to reveal supply chain risks. The user reporting the deficiency must categorize the severity of the consequences to OSS&E; Category I deficiencies are the most serious and could lead to critical failures and loss of life. Table 1.2 describes the categories of deficiency severities.

F. Commodity Council Eight-Step Process for Managing Supply Chain Risks

Figure F.1 summarizes the eight-step commodity council process (Harris, 2004) within which commodity councils manage supply chain risks.

We describe in more depth each step below.

Step 1. Review the Current Strategy: Conduct analysis and research to understand how the commodity is fulfilled today. This includes spend and forecast analysis, supplier analysis for current suppliers, inventory position and strategy, customer feedback, barriers and impediments, etc.

Step 2. Evaluate/Assess the Current Market: Analyze the market to assess trends, emerging or diminishing technologies, and suppliers. All associated tasks are led by the Market Research Analyst in conjunction with the Central Market Research Team.

Step 3. Analyze and Forecast Demands: The goal of this step is to develop a validated supply plan detail and summary based on forecast requirements from D200. It includes

**Figure F.1. Commodity Councils Manage Supply Chain Risk
Within Their Eight-Step Process**

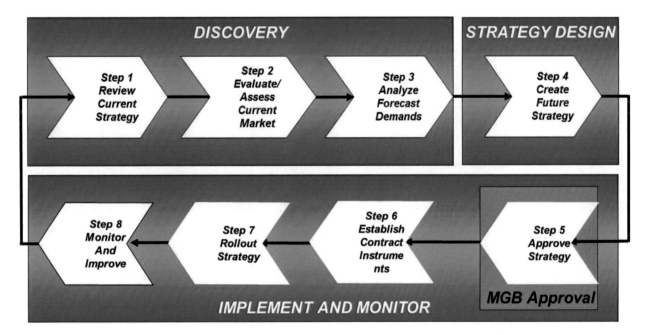

¹Material Governance Board

SOURCE: Logistics Contracting Division (2004).

107

additional concerns from customer input, engineering configuration, spend/forecast variances, supplier capabilities/capacities, and recent developments.

Step 4. Create a Future Strategy: In this step, information from the discovery phase (Steps 1–3) is synthesized to develop potential strategies for the Material Governance Board to consider and approve in Step 5. The output from this step is a Commodity Management Plan (CMP) with recommendations for subcouncils and potential spiral strategies that the council/subcouncils will pursue. Inputs to this step include existing inventory levels and material management and logistics plans. Outputs include key performance indicators and estimates on return on investment. Examples of return on investment include reduced cycle times or improved quality. These outputs also include potential contracting strategies, key milestones, potential barriers, and mitigation plans. The process steps for Step 4 are accomplished at a high level for the CMP and with greater detail in the Commodity Acquisition Management Plan (CAMP).

Step 5. Approve the Strategy: The Material Governance Board considers the CMP and CAMP documents and approves the commodity plan.

Step 6. Establish Contractual Instruments: This step includes the preparation and approval of a performance-based agreement, preparation of a source-selection plan (for competitive contracts), and the issuing of a request for proposal.

Step 7. Roll Out the Strategy: Develop the rules of engagement for the execution of the commodity/supplier strategy. This includes setting up a data-gathering plan to track performance and issuing a user's guide on how to place items on contract and award orders.

Step 8. Monitor and Continuously Improve Strategy and Performance: This step consists of 26 substeps leading to the generation of a variety of reports on compliance and performance. These reports are reviewed by the Materiel Governance Board and used to adjust the commodity strategy and improve supplier performance.

A risk assessment is prescribed under two of the steps (Logistics Contracting Division, 2008). First, Substep 2.4 directs commodity councils to review the supplier's capacity and capabilities (see Figure F.2). This is related to the supplier's ability to meet the demand requirements for the commodity. Technological capability is also considered.

The second place where risk is considered is in Substep 4.6, which calls for a risk assessment of the proposed commodity council purchasing strategy, including risk of meeting the desired goals (see Figure F.3).

Certainly, many of the other steps detailed in the eight-step process are related to risk assessment. For example, Step 2 calls for a market analysis to assess trends, emerging and diminishing technologies and suppliers, etc. Step 2.1.2 calls for the commodity council to obtain industry research reports, including supplier financial data, watch dog reports, and publicly filled reports.

Figure F.2. Market and Capacity Risk Assessed Within Step 2

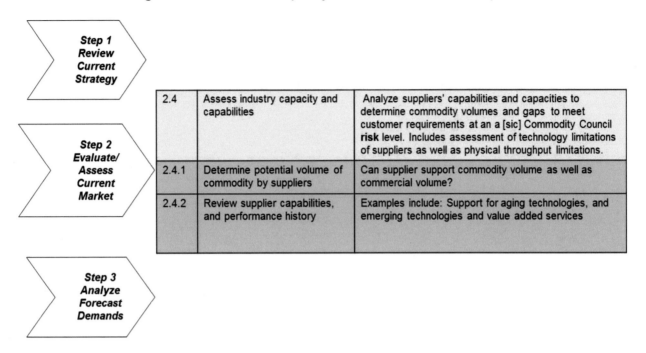

SOURCE: Logistics Contracting Division (2008).

Figure F.3. Output from Capacity Risk Assessment (Step 2) and Demand Forecast (Step 3) Used to Formulate Supply Strategy

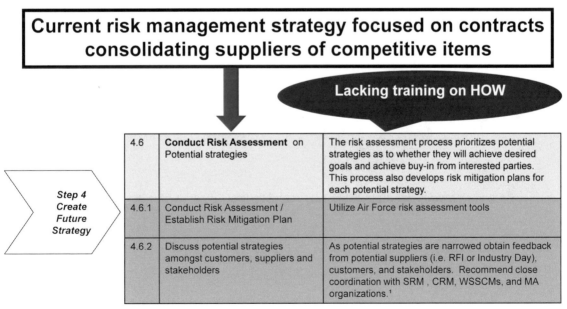

[1] RFI – Request for Information, SRM – Supplier relationship management, CRM - Customer relationship management, WSSCM – Weapon system supply chain manager, MA – Maintenance

SOURCE: Logistics Contracting Division (2008).

Although the commodity council's members were aware of supply chain risks and were sensitive to them, we do not see evidence of an integrated and systematic process for identifying, assessing, or mitigating supply chain risks. We believe that the lack of an integrated approach is due to the commodity councils' emphasis on facilitating contracts. However, it is also due to a lack of training on how to conduct a risk assessment and a belief that the commodity councils do not have enough leverage to change policy or influence supplier behavior. This leads to a narrowly focused approach to supply chain risk management.[37]

---

[37] These findings are based on a conversation with a commodity council lead.

Bibliography

AFI—*See* Air Force Instruction.

Air Force Instruction 10-601, *Operational Capability Requirements Development,* Washington, D.C.: Department of the Air Force, July 31, 2006.

———, 20-101, *Logistics Strategic Planning Procedures,* Washington, D.C.: Department of the Air Force, November 12, 1993. As of October 30, 2012:
http://www.e-publishing.af.mil/shared/media/epubs/AFI20-101.pdf

———, 63-101, *Acquisition and Sustainment Life Cycle Management,* Washington, D.C.: Department of the Air Force, April 8, 2009.

———, 63-501, *Air Force Acquisition Quality Program,* Washington, D.C.: Department of the Air Force, November 4, 2009.

Arena, Mark V., Obaid Younossi, Kevin Brancato, Irv Blickstein, and Clifford A. Grammich, *Why Has the Cost of Fixed-Wing Aircraft Risen? A Macroscopic Examination of the Trends in U.S. Military Aircraft Costs over the Past Several Decades*, Santa Monica, Calif.: RAND Corporation, MG-696-NAVY/AF, 2008. As of July 31, 2012:
http://www.rand.org/pubs/monographs/MG696.html

Berinato, Scott, "What Went Wrong at Cisco in 2001," *CIO*, August 1, 2001. As of November 19, 2013:
http://www.cio.com/article/30413/What_Went_Wrong_at_Cisco_in_2001

Berman, Al, "Business Continuity in a Sarbanes-Oxley World," *Disaster Recovery Journal*, Vol. 17, No. 2, Spring 2004, pp. 14–18.

"Boeing Acquires Stake in Plant," *Wall Street Journal*, December 22, 2009.

Cargille, Brian, and Chris Fry, "Design for Supply Chain: Spreading the Word Across HP," *Supply Chain Management Review*, July/August 2006, pp. 34 ff.

Chenoweth, Mary E., Jeremy Arkes, and Nancy Y. Moore, *Best Practices in Developing Proactive Supply Strategies for Air Force Low-Demand Service Parts,* Santa Monica, Calif.: RAND Corporation, MG-858-AF, 2010. As of November 20, 2013:
http://www.rand.org/pubs/monographs/MG858.html

Chozick, Amy, "Toyota Sticks by 'Just in Time' Strategy After Quake," *Wall Street Journal*, July 24, 2007.

Christopher, Martin, "Understanding Supply Chain Risk: A Self-Assessment Workbook," Bedford, UK: Cranfield University, School of Management, Department for Transport, 2003. As of August 10, 2011:
https://dspace.lib.cranfield.ac.uk/bitstream/1826/4373/1/Understanding_supply_chain_risk.pdf

Cordon, Carlos, "Quality Defaults and Work-in-Process Inventory," *European Journal of Operations Research*, Vol. 80, No. 2, January 1995, pp. 240–251.

Council of Supply Chain Management Professionals, "CSCMP Supply Chain Management Definitions," undated. As of June 15, 2012:
http://cscmp.org/aboutcscmp/definitions.asp

Davidson, Don, "Comprehensive National Cyber Security Initiative & ICT Supply Chain Risk Management," presentation to the National Defense Industrial Association, October 16, 2009. As of September 3, 2011:
http://www.ndia.org/Divisions/Divisions/Logistics/Documents/DD%20at%20NDIA%20Log%2016oct.pdf

Deans, Graeme K., Fritz Kroeger, and Stefan Zeisel, "The Consolidation Curve," *Harvard Business Review*, December 2002, pp. 20–21.

Defense Acquisition University, "Willoughby Templates," February 8, 2012. As of October 30, 2012:
https://bpch.dau.mil/Pages/PracticeView.aspx?pid=413

Defense Acquisition University, "Defense Acquisition Guidebook," June 28, 2013. As of May 22, 2014:
https://acc.dau.mil/CommunityBrowser.aspx?id=654219

Department of Defense, *Defense Acquisition Guidebook,* undated. As of September 1, 2012:
https://acc.dau.mil/dag

———, *Risk Management Guide for DoD Acquisition*, Sixth Edition, August 2006. As of September 1, 2012:
http://www.dau.mil/pubs/gdbks/docs/RMG%206Ed%20Aug06.pdf

———, *Defense Federal Acquisition Regulation Supplement,* 2011. As of September 6, 2011:
http://www.acq.osd.mil/dpap/dars/dfarspgi/current/index.html

Department of Defense Directive (DoDD) 5000.01, *The Defense Acquisition System*, May 12, 2003.

Department of Defense, *Risk Management Guide for DoD Acquisition*, 2006.

Department of Defense Instruction 4140.1-R, *DoD Supply Chain Materiel Management Regulation*, Office of the Deputy Under Secretary of Defense for Logistics and Materiel Readiness, May 23, 2003. As of August 11, 2012:
http://www.dtic.mil/whs/directives/corres/pdf/414001r.pdf

————, 5000.02, *Operation of the Defense Acquisition System,* December 2008.

Department of the Navy, *Best Practices: How to Avoid Surprises in the World's Most Complicated Technical Process: The Transition from Development to Production,* Washington, D.C., March 1986.

DoDD—*See* Department of Defense Directive.

DoDI—*See* Department of Defense Instruction.

Duffy, Roberta, "Supply Base Rationalization," *Critical Issues Report*, CAPS Research, January 2005.

Enslow, Beth, *Stemming the Rising Tide of Supply Chain Risks: How Risk Managers' Roles and Responsibilities Are Changing*, New York: Marsh, April 15, 2008. As of August 2, 2012:
http://usa.marsh.com/Insights/ThoughtLeadership/Articles/ID/539/Stemming-the-Rising-Tide-of-Supply-Chain-Risks-How-Risk-Managers-Roles-and-Responsibilities-Are-Changing.aspx

Favre, Donovan, and John McCreery, "Coming to Grips with Supplier Risk," *Supply Chain Management Review*, September 1, 2008.

Gardner, John T., and Martha C. Cooper, "Strategic Supply Chain Mapping Approaches," *Journal of Business Logistics*, Vol. 24, No. 2, Autumn 2003, pp. 37–64.

"Gates Announces Major Pentagon Priority Shifts," CNN, April 6, 2009. As of August 9, 2011:
http://www.cnn.com/2009/POLITICS/04/06/gates.budget.cuts/index.html

General Accounting Office, *Defense Industry Consolidation and Options for Preserving Competition*, Washington, D.C., GAO/NSAID-98-141, April 1998. As of August 3, 2012:
http://www.gao.gov/archive/1998/ns98141.pdf

Giunipero, Larry C., and Reham Aly Eltantawy, "Securing the Upstream Supply Chain: A Risk Management Approach," *International Journal of Physical Distribution & Logistics Management*, Vol. 34, No. 9, 2004, pp. 698–713.

Griffin, LTCD Wes, "The Future of Integrated Supply Chain Management Utilizing Performance Based Logistics," *Defense Acquisition Review Journal*, Vol. 15, No. 1, April 2008, pp. 3–17. As of July 31, 2012:
http://www.dau.mil/pubscats/PubsCats/ARJ47_Griffin.pdf

113

Hamre, John J., speech to the Council on Foreign Relations, June 5, 1998. As of August 3, 2012:
http://www.defenselink.mil/transcripts/transcript.aspx?transcriptid=1590

Hannon, Dave, "West Coast Ports Back to Normal Activity," *Purchasing*, May 2, 2008.

Harrington, Kevin, and John O'Connor, "How Cisco Succeeds at Global Risk Management," *Supply Chain Management Review*, July/August 2009, pp. 10–17.

Hillman, Mark, and Heather Keltz, *Managing Risk in the Supply Chain—A Quantitative Study*, Boston, Mass.: AMR Research, 2007.

Holmes, Stanley, "Boeing's 787 Encounters Flight Delays," *Business Week*, September 5, 2007.

House Report 1540, National Defense Authorization Act.

International Organization for Standardization, *Risk Management—Vocabulary*, Interim ISO Guide 73, Geneva, Switzerland: ISO, 2009.

Isidore, Chris, "Port Lockout's Bite to Be Felt Soon," *CNN Money*, October 1, 2002. As of August 3, 2012:
http://money.cnn.com/2002/10/01/news/economy/port_impact/

ISO—*See* International Organization for Standardization.

Johnson, Clay III, "Implementing Strategic Sourcing," memorandum for chief acquisition officers, chief financial officers, chief information officers, Washington, D.C.: Office of Management and Budget, May 20, 2005. As of August 3, 2012:
http://www.uspto.gov/web/offices/ac/comp/proc/OMBmemo.pdf

Kempf, Edward, "Sustainment Commodity Councils Overview," Air Force Sustainment Center, 429 SCMS/GUBB briefing, October 31, 2012.

Kim, Chang-Ran, "Toyota Says Supply Chain Will Be Ready by August for Next Quake," Reuters, March 2, 2012. As of March 2, 2012:
http://uk.reuters.com/article/2012/03/02/uk-toyota-supply-chain-idUKTRE8210BW20120302

Kiser, James, and George Cantrell, "6 Steps to Managing Risk," *Supply Chain Management Review*, April 2006, pp. 12-17.

Latour, Almar, "Trial by Fire: A Blaze in Albuquerque Sets off Major Crisis for Cell-Phone Giants," *Wall Street Journal*, January 29, 2001.

LCP Consulting in conjunction with the Centre for Logistics and Supply Chain Management, *Understanding Supply Chain Risk: A Self-Assessment Workbook*, Bedford, UK: Cranfield University Centre for Logistics and Supply Chain Management, 2003.

Lee, Han L., V. Padmanabhan, and Seungjin Whang, "The Bullwhip Effect in Supply Chains," *Sloan Management Review*, Vol. 38, No. 3, Spring 1997, pp. 93–102.

Levin, Carl, "Summary of the Weapon Systems Acquisition Reform Act of 2009," February 24, 2009. As of September 3, 2011:
http://levin.senate.gov/newsroom/press/release/?id=fc5cf7a4-47b2-4a72-b421-ce324a939ce4

Linstone, Harold A., and Murray Turoff, eds., *The Delphi Method: Techniques and Applications*, 2002. As of August 7, 2012:
http://is.njit.edu/pubs/delphibook/

Logistics Contracting Division, "Eight Step Process," AFMC spend analysis capabilities briefing, HQ AFMC/LGK, August 11, 2004.

Logistics Contracting Division, "CC_8_Step_Process_WBS(6).xls," Microsoft Excel file, June 16, 2008.

Lynn, William J., Deputy Secretary of Defense, "Directive-Type Memorandum (DTM) 09-016—Supply Chain Risk Management (SCRM) to Improve the Integrity of Components Used in DoD Systems," March 25, 2010, Incorporating Change 3, March 23, 2012. As of June 20, 2012:
http://www.dtic.mil/whs/directives/corres/pdf/DTM-09-016.pdf

Magretta, Joan, "The Power of Virtual Integration: An Interview with Dell Computer's Michael Dell," *Harvard Business Review*, March–April 1998, pp. 72–85.

McKenna, J., "ILWU Contract on West Coast and Possible Impacts on Ports and Congestion," speech at the 2007 Real Estate Logistics Forum, Dallas, Tex., June 11, 2007.

Moore, Nancy Y., and Elvira N. Loredo, *Identifying and Managing Air Force Sustainment Supply Chain Risks*, Santa Monica, Calif.: RAND Corporation, DB-649-AF, 2013. As of November 21, 2013:
http://www.rand.org/pubs/documented_briefings/DB649.html

Mulligan, Jan, "Ensuring an Adequate Infrastructure to Execute Assigned Maintenance Workload," briefing, Washington, D.C.: Headquarters United States Air Force, Office of Logistics, Installations and Mission Support, November 15, 2007. As of July 31, 2012:
http://www.sae.org/events/dod/presentations/2007janmulligan.pdf

National Atlas of the United States, 2012. As of October 30, 2012:
http://nationalatlas.gov

Nelson, Dave, Rick Mayo, and Patricia E. Moody, *Powered by Honda: Developing Excellence in the Global Enterprise*, New York: John Wiley & Sons, 1998.

Norrman, Andreas, and Ulf Jansson, "Ericsson's Proactive Supply Chain Risk Management Approach After a Serious Sub-Supplier Accident," *International Journal of Physical Distribution and Logistics Management,* Vol. 34, No. 5, 2004, pp. 434–456.

O'Connor, John, "Supply Chain Risk Management: Cisco Systems," presented to Council of Supply Chain Management Professionals (CSCMP) Annual Global Conference, Denver, Colo., October 2008.

Office of Management and Budget, Circular A-76, *Revised Supplemental Handbook,* Washington, D.C., June 14, 1999.

———, *The President's Management Agenda for FY 2002,* Washington, D.C., 2001.

Office of the Under Secretary of Defense for Acquisition, Technology, and Logistics, *Report of the Defense Science Board Task Force on Mission Impact of Foreign Influence on DoD Software,* September 2007. As of August 3, 2012:
http://www.acq.osd.mil/dsb/reports/ADA486949.pdf

Office of the Under Secretary of Defense, Comptroller, *National Defense Budget Estimates for FY 2013,* March 2012. As of August 3, 2012:
http://comptroller.defense.gov/defbudget/fy2013/FY13_Green_Book.pdf

OMB—*See* Office of Management and Budget.

Payton, Sue C., "Guidance Memorandum: Life Cycle Risk Management," November 4, 2008.

Peck, Helen, Martin Christopher, Jennifer Abley, et al., *Creating Resilient Supply Chains: A Practical Guide,* Bedford, UK: Cranfield University School of Management, Department for Transport, 2003.

Perry, William J., *Annual Report to the President and Congress,* Secretary of Defense, Washington, D.C., March 1996.

Public Law 105-270, Federal Activities Inventory Reform Act of 1998, 105th Congress.

Public Law 111-8, Omnibus Appropriations Act, 2009, March 11, 2009. As of October 23, 2012:
http://www.gpo.gov/fdsys/pkg/PLAW-111publ8/pdf/PLAW-111publ8.pdf

"Questions for Maj Gen McMahon—LOA," October 14, 2008. As of September 3, 2011:
http://www.docstoc.com/docs/36357159/Questions-for-Maj-Gen-McMahon-%E2%80%93-LOA_-14-Oct-08

Rooney, Jo Ann, Acting Under Secretary of Defense, Personnel and Readiness, Memorandum: "Update on OMB Circular A-76 Public Private Competition Prohibitions," March 8, 2012.

Samsung Data Systems America, "Design for Supply Chain," undated. As of August 8, 2012:
http://www.scribd.com/doc/80605254/Design-for-Supply-Chain

Schellhorn, Gerhard, Andreas Thums, and Wolfgang Reif, "Formal Fault Tree Semantics," in H. Ehrig, B. J. Kramer, and A. Ertas, eds., *Proceedings of the Sixth World Conference on Integrated Design and Process Technology*, Pasadena, Calif., June 2002, pp. 1-8.

SCRLC—*See* Supply Chain Risk Leadership Council.

Secretary of the Air Force, *USAF Deficiency Reporting, Investigation and Resolution,* TO-00-35D-54, 2011.

Sheffi, Yosef, *The Resilient Enterprise: Overcoming Vulnerability for Competitive Advantage*, Cambridge, Mass.: MIT Press, 2005.

Sheffi, Yossi, and James B. Rice, Jr., "A Supply Chain View of the Resilient Enterprise," *MIT Sloan Management Review,* Vol. 47, No. 1, Fall 2005, pp. 41–48. As of July 31, 2012: http://sloanreview.mit.edu/the-magazine/2005-fall/47110/a-supply-chain-view-of-the-resilient-enterprise/

Smith, Briony, "Intel: Disasters Can Be 'Business as Usual' with Enough Planning," *ComputerWorld*, June 18, 2008. As of August 3, 2012: http://www.computerworld.com/s/article/9100518/Intel_Disasters_can_be_business_as_usual_with_enough_planning

Solomon, Lance, and Joe McMorrow, "Case Study: Chengdu Earthquake Crisis Response," *Supply Chain Risk Leadership Council Newsletter,* Fourth Quarter, 2008. As of August 3, 2012: http://www.scrlc.com/newsletter-readMore.php?aID=134

Steele, Paul T., and Brian H. Court, *Profitable Purchasing Strategies: A Manager's Guide for Improving Organizational Competitiveness Through the Skills of Purchasing*, London: McGraw-Hill, 1996.

Supply Chain Risk Leadership Council, "Supply Chain Risk Management: A Compilation of Best Practices," August 2011. As of March 17, 2014: http://www.scrlc.com/articles/Supply_Chain_Risk_Management_A_Compilation_of_Best_Practices_final[1].pdf

Supply Chain Risk Leadership Council, "Supply Chain Risk Maturity Model," April 2, 1013. As of March 17, 2014: http://www.scrlc.com/

"The 11 Greatest Supply Chain Disasters," *SupplyChainDigest*, 2006. As of November 20,2013: http://www.scdigest.com/assets/reps/SCDigest_Top-11-SupplyChainDisasters.pdf

Thompson, Mark, "Can Robert Gates Tame the Pentagon," *Time*, February 12, 2009. As of July 31, 2012: http://www.time.com/time/magazine/article/0,9171,1879176,00.html

Van De Ven, Andrew H., and André L. Delbecq, "The Effectiveness of Nominal, Delphi, and Interacting Group Decision Making Processes," *The Academy of Management Journal*, Vol. 17, No. 4, December 1974, pp. 605–621.

Verstraete, Christian, "Share and Share Alike," *Supply Chain Quarterly,* Quarter 2, 2008. As of August 6, 2012:
http://www.supplychainquarterly.com/topics/Global/scq200802risk/

White House, "Memorandum on Government Contracting," March 4, 2009. As of October 29, 2012:
http://www.whitehouse.gov/the_press_office/Memorandum-for-the-Heads-of-Executive-Departments-and-Agencies-Subject-Government

Wieland, Andreas, and Carl Marcus Wallenburg, "Dealing with Supply Chain Risks," *International Journal of Physical Distribution and Logistics Management*, Vol. 42, No. 10, November 2012, pp. 887–905.

World Trade Organization, *World Trade Report 2008: Trade in a Globalizing World,* 2008. As of August 2, 2012:
http://www.wto.org/english/res_e/reser_e/wtr08_e.htm

Yates, J. Frank, and Eric R. Stone, "Risk Appraisal," in J. Frank Yates, ed., *Risk Taking Behavior*, New York: John Wiley & Sons, 1992, pp. 48–86.

Ziegenbein, Arne, and Jörg Nienhaus, "Coping with Supply Chain Risks on Strategic, Tactical, and Operational Levels," in Richard J. Harvey, ed., *Global Project and Manufacturing Management Symposium Proceedings*, May 2004, Siegen, Germany: MIP, 2004.

Zsidisin, George A., Alex Panelli, and Rebecca Upton, "Purchasing Organization Involvement in Risk Assessments, Contingency Plans, and Risk Management: An Exploratory Study," *Supply Chain Management*, Vol. 5, No. 4, 2000, pp. 187–198.

Zsidisin, George, Gary L. Ragatz, and Steve A. Melnyk, "Effective Practices for Business Continuity Planning in Purchasing and Supply Management: A Management White Paper," Department of Marketing and Supply Chain Management, East Lansing, Mich.: Eli Broad Graduate School of Management, Michigan State University, July 21, 2003.

Zsidisin, George, Gary L. Ragatz, and Steve A. Melnyk, "The Dark Side of Supply Chain Management," *Supply Chain Management Review*, March 2005, pp. 46–52.